"This very useful book a   just a few pages.

"First, it provides a good basic introduction to Austin Spare's system with a proper explanation of its place in Western magical thought.

"Next, it contains a straightforward and comprehensive account of a number of very practical magical techniques, going beyond Spare's work to include some state-of-the-art developments.

"Finally, even for the magician with no direct interest in Spare or sigil magic, the whole subject is discussed in an intelligent way, which provokes one to think again and again about magic, its operation and its principles.

"I look forward to further work from Frater U∴D∴ because it reflects something truly important: in astrological terms, he seems able to bring together the *cardinality* of British magical thinking with the *fixity* of German application to create a magical current that is at last *mutable* in the sense that it's alive, it's fertile, and it's going somewhere."

—LIONEL SNELL (RAMSEY DUKES)
Thundersqueak

"Frater U∴D∴ introduces us to a remarkable discipline— sigil magic. Providing practical techniques and explaining in detail the underlying psychological principles involved, he has opened the way for a magical restructuring of one's own inner universe. Using the works of Austin Osman Spare, he develops the system into a 21st-century model of magical practice by avoiding Old Aeon concepts as "High," "Low," "Black," or "White" magic, offering instead a new magical perspective—Pragmatic Magic.

"This system requires hard work but will provide definite results. Frater U∴D∴, like Pete Carroll and Lionel Snell amongst others, is part of a new generation of Magicians dragging the occult world screaming and kicking into the New Aeon."

—FREYA
Northern Mysteries & Magick

Practical
Sigil Magic

About the Author

Frater U.·.D.·., otherwise known as Ralph Tegtmeier, is a foremost practitioner and expert of modern Pragmatic Magic. Born in Egypt, he studied Eastern philosophy for many years before delving into the principles of Western magic. Previously an occult bookseller, he holds a master's degree in Comparative Literature and is a prolific writer and translator. His work has been published in *The Lamp of Thoth and Chaos International*. Frater U.·.D.·. founded *Anubis*, a German magazine of practical magic and psychonautics and has translated Peter Carroll's *Liber Null & Psychonaut* and Aleister Crowley's *Book of Lies* into German.

Practical
Sigil Magic

Creating Personal
Symbols for Success

Frater U∴D∴

Translated from German by Ingrid Fischer
Revised and enlarged special edition for the Americas

Llewellyn Publications
Woodbury, Minnesota

SECOND EDITION
Second Printing, 2013

Cover design by Lisa Novak
Cover illustration © Gary Hanna
Interior illustrations by the Llewellyn Art Department

Llewellyn Publications is a registered trademark of Llewellyn Worldwide Ltd.

Library of Congress Cataloging-in-Publication Data
U.D., Frater, 1952–
    [Sigillenmagie in der Praxis. English]
    Practical Sigil Magic / by Frater U.D. ; translated from German by Ingrid Fischer.—Rev. and enl. special ed. for the Americas.
       p.   cm. — (Llewellyn's practical magick series)
    Translation of: Sigillenmagie in der Praxis.
    Includes bibliographical references.
    ISBN: 978-0-7387-3153-7
    1. Magic.   2. Sigils.   I. Title.   II. Series.
BF1623.S5U32   1990
133.4'3—dc20   89-78492
                                                                      CIP

Llewellyn Worldwide Ltd. does not participate in, endorse, or have any authority or responsibility concerning private business transactions between our authors and the public.

All mail addressed to the author is forwarded, but the publisher cannot, unless specifically instructed by the author, give out an address or phone number.

Any Internet references contained in this work are current at publication time, but the publisher cannot guarantee that a specific location will continue to be maintained. Please refer to the publisher's website for links to authors' websites and other sources.

Llewellyn Publications
A Division of Llewellyn Worldwide Ltd.
2143 Wooddale Drive
Woodbury, MN 55125-2989
www.llewellyn.com

Printed in the United States of America

Other Books by this author

Money Magic

High Magic

High Magic II

Where Do Demons Live?

Contents

Introduction . . . 1

Chapter 1: Austin Osman Spare and
   His Theory of Sigils . . . 7

Chapter 2: Further Exploration of the
   Word Method . . . 19

Chapter 3: The Magical Trance / Activating
   the Sigils . . . 35

Chapter 4: The Pictorial Method . . . 49

Chapter 5: The Mantrical Spell Method . . . 59

Chapter 6: The Alphabet of Desire . . . 67

Chapter 7: Working with Atavistic Nostalgia . . . 87

Chapter 8: But How Does It Work? . . . 97

Chapter 9: Constructing Sigils with
   Planetary Cameas . . . 107

Conclusion . . . 127
Glossary . . . 129
Comments . . . 133
Bibliography . . . 139

Introduction

Sigil magic, particularly the system developed by the English painter and sorcerer Austin Osman Spare, is one of the most efficient and economical disciplines of magic. For the most part, it can be performed without complicated rituals, needs hardly any paraphernalia, is independent of philosophical and dogmatic premises and, due to its simplicity, can be learned easily and quickly. Most important of all, *none of the magical techniques we know of today is more efficient and will give even beginners the immediate chance to convince themselves of its power and their own abilities.* These reasons alone support a volume like the following to show the possibilities of this discipline and to explain its techniques and its rationale. The reader—the complete tyro and the advanced practitioner alike—will receive an introduction which will accompany him/her in his/her magical practice for a long time to come.

You will find in this edition, in the following chapter, a reprint of my article "Austin Osman Spare and His Theory of Sigils" from the, alas, now-defunct German magazine *Unicorn*, issue 1/82. This issue has been out of print for quite some time, but many readers' inquiries have shown that there is still much interest in this article, and it is increasing every day. Since the article also covers some of the historical and philosophical background of Spare's sigil magic, it might be useful to present it here within a new context to a greater audience.

The *word method* explained in the article will be shown in greater depth in chapter 2. Further examples will be given, as well as comments and tips for practical use which you will rarely find in literature on this subject.

Next we will deal with the *pictorial method,* which has several advantages and disadvantages when compared to the word method. Again, in accordance with the title of this volume, magical practice will be of primary importance.

A description of the *mantrical spell method* will complete the techniques of sigil construction proper. It is my hope that examples and commentaries from my personal practice will provide you with many new suggestions.

Although Spare's mysterious *Alphabet of Desire* belongs, technically speaking, to the pictorial method and in some respects touches the word method, it may nevertheless be considered the center of his magical achievement. Unfortunately, his own comments about it are rather vague. Therefore, most writers, being familiar with the subject on a theoretical level only, have caused much confusion rather than clarity when discussing it. Yet, it seems to me that the basic principle of this magical symbol language is amazingly simple if viewed in relation to Spare's system as a whole.

The chapter "The Alphabet of Desire," therefore, will not only offer a cursory comment on fragments from Spare's rather chaotic legacy but introduce a mature system of symbol-logic, accessible to everyone. This certainly would have been Spare's intent had he ever finished what has become known as the legendary *Grimoire of Zos,* i.e., had he completed it with explanatory comments for the magicians of his time.

Albeit Spare's personal philosophy (which he himself termed the *Zos Kia Cultus*) is not that important for sigil magic itself, we should not fail to mention his technique of *Atavistic nostalgia,* which is certainly one of the most fascinating applications of sigil magic. Furthermore, it marks its connection to Shamanism and so-called "primitive magic," two disciplines from which today's magicians can only profit.

The main topic of the last chapter will concern *planetary sigils* from the Hermetic Tradition. Although experts have been familiar with the method of their construction for decades, little or no relevant literature has as yet been made available to a wider public. It, therefore, seemed pertinent to treat this subject matter here.

The reader will note that in this volume we concentrate on creating *personal*, that is to say, *individual* sigils. This is a completely different approach compared to the tendency of many other books, which usually prefer to list traditional, largely mutilated or inaccurately reproduced sigils taken from the "magical cookbooks" of generally obscure authors with little or no practical experience of their own. Although the planetary sigils discussed at the end of this study are taken from the work of Agrippa of Nettesheim, who is above all criticism in this respect, a single glance at other standard works about magical symbols will show that most magicians and alchemists in the Middle Ages (the supposed "peak" of Occidental magic) largely developed their own sigil language using a rather small number of well-established symbols. The myth that there is a small number of "correct" sigils and a great variety of "wrong" ones for entities (generally demons), whose names are often little else but mutilations of misunderstood older terms,[1] has confused the minds of even highly experienced old hands. Such misinformation should no longer be tolerated.

Of course, even "wrong" dogmas can develop their own, definitely real, magical egregore in the course of time. But we should no longer be interested in struggling with the astral garbage which others have been creating for centuries. Spare has certainly opened—probably without an expressed intention to do so—our eyes to an atavism different from the one discussed in chapter 6, for he has shown us the origin of all magical symbolism—the *human soul itself!* His message is that those magical sigils which truly work derive from our own unconscious and will return again to their source to begin their work after being impregnated by our will. Naturally, and this applies to all magic, one might gain the false impression that it would be much less of a strain to get everything organized and prepared straight from the horse's mouth of a "Great Illuminated True Master of Wisdom," but this has nothing to do whatsoever with practical magical success. One could compare this to studying at a university: anything you may have missed in the beginning through idleness will have to be made up for in the end with triple effort. But, you usually don't have enough time to catch up.

Spare states that "sigils are monograms of thought" and that they should be created in accordance with the individuality of our thinking. So please, view the examples given in this study for what they are—examples only. Don't use them lazily and heedlessly. This could definitely be dangerous! At the beginning you will need perhaps a quarter of an hour or so for your first individual sigil, but by your fifth or sixth sigil it will take you only a couple of minutes. This effort will certainly prove to be worthwhile if you consider the probable success.

As I said before, sigil magic is probably one of those magical disciplines that may be the fastest and easiest to learn. Usually, you will need nothing more than a sheet of paper and a pen. With some experience, you will have finished the whole operation, including activation and subsequent banishing, within less than five to ten minutes. There is no faster way—even in magic!

Chapter 1

Austin Osman Spare and His Theory of Sigils[2]

The end of the nineteenth and the beginning of the twentieth century was a time characterized by radical changes and great heretics. The secret lore and the occult in general were triumphant, and there were good reasons for this: the triumph of materialist positivism with its Manchester industrialism was beginning to show its first malice, resulting in social and psychological uprooting; the destruction of nature had already begun to bear its first poisonous fruits. In brief, it was a time when it seemed appropriate to question the belief in technology and the omnipotence of the celebrated natural sciences. Particularly intellectuals, artists, and the so-called "Bohemians" became advocates of values critical of civilization in general as can be seen in the literature of Naturalism, in Expressionist Art and in the whole Decadent Movement, which was quite notorious at the time.

Austin Osman Spare (1886–1956) was a typical child of this era and, after Aleister Crowley, he was definitely one of the most interesting occultists and practicing magicians of the English-speaking world. Nowadays he is basically known only in this cultural context;[3] internationally, he has received only some attention in literary circles at best—ironically, in a footnote! This footnote is found in Mario Praz's pioneering but, unfortunately, rather superficial work *La carne, la morte e il diavolo nella letteratura romantica (The Romantic Agony,* Florence, 1930) where he terms him, together with Aleister Crowley, a "satanic occultist"[4]—and that is all. Nevertheless, this important work has at least led many an occult researcher familiar with literature to Spare.

Compared with Aleister Crowley's enigmatic and infamous life, Austin Osman Spare's existence certainly seemed to befit only a footnote. Despite his various publications after the turn of the century, he remained practically unnoticed until the late sixties.

He was born in 1886, the son of a London police officer, and we know very little about his childhood. He claimed to have experienced, while a child, an initiation of sorts by an elderly witch, one Mrs. Paterson who, as far as we know, must have been quite a Wiccan-like character. Spare found his intellectual and creative vocation as an artist and illustrator, and he attended the Royal College of Art, where he soon was celebrated as a forthcoming young artist. But he rebelled against a bourgeois middle-class career in the arts. Disgusted by commercialism, he retreated from the artistic scene soon afterwards, though he still continued editing various magazines for quite a while. From 1927 until his death, he virtually lived as a weird hermit in a London slum, where he sometimes held exhibitions in a local pub.

People have compared his life with that of H. P. Lovecraft, and certainly he too was an explorer of the dark levels of the soul. Around the beginning of the First World War, he released some privately published editions, and today one can acquire—at least in Great Britain—numerous, usually highly expensive, reprints of his works. However, we are primarily interested in two volumes, namely his well-known *Book of Pleasure (Self-Love): The Psychology of Ecstasy* (London, 1913)[5] and Kenneth Grant's excellently researched book[6] in which he, as leader of his own brand of O.T.O. *(Ordo Templi Orientis)* and as an expert on Crowley, deals with the practical aspects of Spare's system as well. Spare's actual philosophy will not be analyzed in depth here because this is not really necessary for the practice of sigil theory and it would lead away from the subject of this study.

Before we begin with Spare's theory of sigils, it is perhaps useful to write a few words about the part sigils play in a magical working. Occidental magic is known to rest on two main pillars, namely on *will* and on *imagination*. Connected with these are analogous thinking and symbolic images. For example, Agrippa uses a special sigil for each of the planetary intelligences. These are not, as has been assumed for quite some time, arbitrarily constructed, nor were they received by "revelation," but rather they are based on cabbalistic considerations.[7]

The Hermetic Order of the Golden Dawn also employed sigils as "images of the souls" of magical entities, which enabled the magician to establish contact with them; nevertheless, the technique of their construction was not explained. The same may be said for the O.T.O. under Crowley's leadership and for the *Fraternitas Saturni* under Gregorius.

The name *Agrippa* already hints at the fact that magical sigils have a long historical tradition, which we will not discuss here because then we would have to cover the whole complex of occult iconology as well. In general, people think of "correct" and "incorrect" sigils. The grimoires of the late Middle Ages were often little else but "magical recipe books" (the frequently criticized *Sixth and Seventh Books of Moses* basically applies the same procedure of "select ingredients, pour in and stir"), and these practitioners believed in the following principle: to know the "true" name and the "true" sigil of a demon means to have power over it.

Pragmatic Magic, which developed in the Anglo-Saxon realms, completely tidied up this concept.[8] Often Crowley's revolt in the Golden Dawn—at first in favor of but soon against Mathers—is seen as the actual beginning of modern magic. It would certainly not be wrong to say that Crowley himself was an important supporter of Pragmatic thought in modern magic. But in the end, the Master Therion preferred to remain within the hierarchical Dogmatic system due to his Aiwass-revelation in *Liber*

Al vel Legis. His key phrase "Do what thou wilt shall be the whole of the Law. Love is the law, love under will," as well as his whole Thelemic concept, prove him a Dogmatic magician.

Not so Austin Osman Spare. He seems to derive from the individual-anarchistic direction so that we may describe his philosophy, without undue exaggeration, as a mixture of Lao-Tse, Wicca, and Max Stirner.

English magic of the turn of the century was also influenced by an important young science which would actually achieve its major triumphs only after the Second World War—the psychology of Sigmund Freud. Before that, Blavatsky's *Isis Unveiled* and *The Secret Doctrine,* as well as Frazer's *The Golden Bough,* had given important impulses to the occult in general. William James' comparative psychology of religion influenced deeply the intellectuality of this time, but Freud, Adler, and especially Carl G. Jung eventually effected major breakthroughs. From then on, people started to consider the unconscious in earnest.

This apparent digression, which had to be kept very short due to lack of space, is in reality a very important basis for the discussion that follows. We will not analyze in depth by whom Spare was influenced. Lao-Tse and Stirner having already been mentioned, we might note numerous others from Swinburne to Crowley himself, in whose order, the A.·.A.·., Spare had been a member at least for a short while. Rather, we will discuss his greatest achievement—his psychological approach towards magic.

This leads us to magical practice proper. In Spare's system there are no "correct" or "incorrect" sigils; neither is there a list of ready-made symbols. It is of no import whether a sigil is the "correct" one or not, but it *is* crucial that it has been created by the magician and is therefore meaningful to him/her. Because s/he has constructed it for personal use, the sigil easily becomes a catalyst of his/her magical desire, and sometimes it will even waken this desire in the first place. This Pragmatic approach which dominates present-day Anglo-Saxon magic (Israel Regardie, Francis King, Stephen Skinner, W. B. Gray, David Conway, Lemuel Johnstone, to name but a few relevant authors) goes to show that Austin Osman Spare, rather than Aleister Crowley, should be considered the real Father of modern Pragmatic Magic.[9]

In the German-speaking countries, the situation is quite different. Writers like Quintscher, Gregorius, Bardon, Klingsor and even Spiesberger allow but little room to maneuver when creating magical coordinates individually. Here the adept is expected to grow into a ready-made system instead of fashioning one. This is a completely different approach, the value or non-value of which we will not discuss here. The nearest thing to Pragmatic Magic, existing already in 1917 i.e. 1921 (the date of the second revised edition of his major work on magic as an experimental science), was Staudenmaier. The works by Mahamudra, which have received some attention, are mainly of a descriptive nature and deal with traditions and new interpretations, thus remaining within the context of German magical heritage; however, they do take heed of recent results in scientific psychology and are, therefore, at least partially related to the Pragmatic approach.

Pragmatic Magic will become more and more important because today's magicians have to face a psychologized—

and psychologizing—environment whose philosophical relativism has been shaping all of us, and still does. Regardless of the significance or amount of truth one concedes to psychology/psychoanalysis, we all are infiltrated by its way of thinking and its vocabulary. So even we magicians will have to attain to a critical, sensible look at it. It will be left to another era to find different models of explanation, description, and practice.

How does Spare proceed in practice? Sigils are developed by fusion and stylization of letters (see Figure 1).

First of all, a sentence of desire has to be formulated. Let us take the example Spare himself gives in his *Book of Pleasure,* the declaration of intent:

THIS MY WISH TO OBTAIN
THE STRENGTH OF A TIGER

This sentence must be written down in capitals. Next, all the letters which appear more than once are deleted so that only one of each letter remains.

THIS MY W̸I̸S̸H̸ T̸O O̸B̸T̸A̸I̸N
T̸H̸E S̸T̸R̸E̸N̸G̸T̸H̸ O̸F A̸ T̸I̸G̸E̸R̸

Thus, the following letters remain: T, H, I, S, M, Y, W, O, B, A, N, E, R, G, F. The sigil is created from these letters; it is permissible to consider one part (for example, M) as a reversed W or, seen from the side, as an E. Hence, these three letters do not have to appear in the sigil three separate times. Of course, there are numerous possibilities of representation and stylization.

"This my wish to obtain the strength of a tiger."

Sigilized this would be:

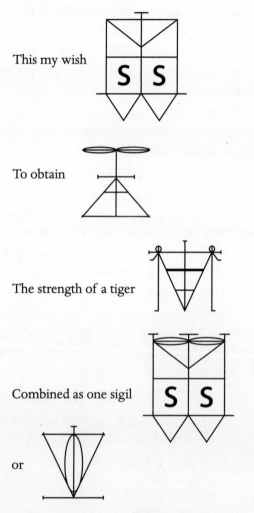

This my wish

To obtain

The strength of a tiger

Combined as one sigil

or

Figure 1

However, it is important that in the end the sigil is as simple as possible with the various letters recognizable (even with slight difficulty). The artistic quality of the sigil is irrelevant, but for simple psychological reasons it should be obvious that you should not just scribble or doodle it in haste. You should strive to make it to the best of your abilities.

The finished sigil, which in the beginning will probably take a few attempts to construe, will then be fixated. You may draw it on parchment, on paper, in the sand, or even on a wall. According to Spare's short instructions, it should be destroyed after its internalization. Thus, you will either burn the parchment, wipe it out in the sand, etc. Spare's basic idea is that the sigil, together with its meaning, must be planted into the unconscious. Afterwards, the consciousness has to forget it so that the unconscious can obey its encoded direction without hindrance.

Formulating the sentence of desire[10] and drawing the sigil should be done with the utmost concentration. It makes the following activation ("charging") much easier.

When the sigil is ready, it is activated by implanting it into the psyche. This is the most difficult part in this process, and Spare offers only very few hints on practical procedures. However, it is crucial that the sigil is internalized in a trance of sorts. This may take place in a state of euphoria (for example, by means of drugs), in ecstasy (for example, sex magically by masturbation, sexual intercourse or a ritual), or in a state of physical fatigue. For the latter example, eyes and arms may be tired by the magician folding his/her arms behind the head while standing in front of a mirror and staring fixedly at his/her image.

The important thing is that it should *click*, meaning that the sigil must be internalized spasmodically, which, of course, requires some exercise and control. This procedure may be supported by repeating the sentence of desire rhythmically and monotonously like a mantra, becoming faster and faster; in doing so, one must stare fixedly at the sigil. (In our example of looking into the mirror [a magical mirror may be used, too], it is useful to draw the sigil onto the mirror with water-soluble paint.)

After spasmodical internalization, the symbol must be destroyed and deleted from the conscious mind. As mentioned before, from now on it will be the unconscious which has to do the work.

In my own practical work I have discovered that it may even be useful to keep the sigil on you, such as wearing a ring engraved with it, etc. But this will depend upon the magician's individual predilection, and everybody should find his/her own way. Occasionally, it may prove necessary to repeat the whole procedure, especially if the goal is a very problematical one, requiring an outstanding amount of energy. Nevertheless, experience shows that it is of prime importance not to bring back the meaning and aim of the sigil into consciousness at any time. We are, after all, dealing with a technique akin to autosuggestion; thus, the rules are the same as with autosuggestions themselves. Therefore, you may not use negative formulas such as "THIS MY WISH NOT TO ..." because very often the unconscious tends neither to recognize nor understand this "not," and you might end up getting the opposite result than that which you originally desired. If you see a sigil every day, perhaps on a wall or engraved on the outer side of a ring, this should only take place unconsciously, just as one might not consciously notice an object which is in use all the time. Of course, you should keep your operation secret, for discussing it with skeptics or even good friends may dissolve the sigil's power.

The advantages of this method, of which only a short summary can be given here, are obvious. It is temptingly easy, and with only a little practice it may be performed at any time and at any place. It does not call for any costly paraphernalia; protective Circles and Pentagram rituals are not required (though sometimes they may prove useful, especially with operations of magical protection), etc.

People who tend toward psychic instability should, however, be cautious. Although the threshold of schizophrenia is not as easily crossed with this method as with common evocations, it does involve cutting deeply into the ecology of the psyche, an act which should be considered carefully in any case. The psycho-magical consequences are sometimes quite incalculable. As is well known, the real problem with magic is not so much the question of *whether* it works, but rather the fact that it *does*.

Used with responsibility, this method offers the magician a tool which provides him/her with a limitless variety of possible magical applications.

Chapter 2

Further Exploration
of the Word Method

The article "Austin Osman Spare and His Theory of Sigils," contained in the last chapter, has already covered the basic principles and background of sigil magic, but it could not go into more depth due to the limited space characteristic of magazine articles. Also, Spare's sigil magic has seen some further evolution during recent years, especially by English Chaos magicians as manifested in the various publications of the IOT order (IOT today = *The Magical Pact of the Illuminates of Thanateros*). Thus, ever-growing divergences from Spare's own methods and intentions have become quite common.

To illustrate the *word method* (i.e., the construction of sigils employing the letters and words of a sentence of desire), Figure 1 of the preceding chapter gives some examples. The whole procedure occurs as follows:

1. The *sentence of desire* must be formulated and written down in capital letters.
2. *Repeated letters are deleted so that every letter will be used but once.*
3a. *Several parts of the sentence are sigilized into several single sigils.*

OR:

3b. All letters of the *whole sentence* are combined into *one general sign.*

4a. *Single sigils* are combined into *one general sigil.*

OR:

4b. The general sigil constructed in 3b is simplified/stylized.

5. The sigil is *internalized/activated.* (Specific techniques are discussed in the following chapter.)
6. The sigil is *banished* and *forgotten.* (Specific techniques are discussed in the following chapter.)

Further Examples for Constructing Sigils Using the Word Method

a) Using the same sentence as in chapter 1, "THIS MY WISH TO OBTAIN THE STRENGTH OF A TIGER," the following letters remain after deleting all double or multiple ones: T, H, I, S, M, Y, W, O, B, A, N, E, R, G, F.

THIS MY WISH (T, H, I, S, M, Y, W)

TO OBTAIN (O, B, A, N)

THE STRENGTH OF
A TIGER (E, R, G, F)

Combined into one general sigil:

or:

b) You may also form all the letters of the whole sentence
(again without any repeats) into one general sigil, avoiding the construction of several single sigils.

The letter E ($\in$), for instance, may be seen as W ($\cup$)
as well as an M ($\cap$). See Figures 2 and 3.

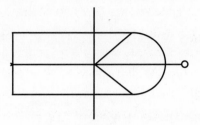

Figure 2

Figure 3

With a little bit of experience, you will be able to combine steps 3 and 4 into one single operation, especially if you have developed your own personal artistic "sigil style." A. O. Spare, who practiced this technique throughout all of his life, had an advantage over the average sigil drawer because he was a highly talented and acknowledged artist who could develop very beautiful and attractive sigils. *But artistic talent is no criterion for the success of sigil magic! THE MOST IMPORTANT POINT IS THAT YOU CREATE THE SIGILS FOR YOURSELF.*

Our glyphs may even look a bit "ugly," "primitive," "roughhewn" or "handmade," and sometimes this may even be an added bonus. Because of their "unrefined" image, they will appear to our unconscious (which will have to struggle with them) much more "magical" or maybe just "less ordinary." In other words, a so-called "ugly" sigil differs a lot from our standardized and smoothed-up everyday environment of glossy machines and industrial pseudo-aesthetics. Since we are working with *Magis,* or the original magical power which belongs, according to current theories, to a praeter-conscious, i.e., "primitive" stage of being, everything which reminds us of the times of amateurish handicraft will awaken primordial impulses in our reptilian brain. This will virtually automatically liberate the magical power in this section of the brain or awaken it in the first place.

Of course, all this depends largely on the magician's personal paradigm. So place your trust in your feelings (i.e., your intuition) rather than in rules which other magicians have set up according to their own subjective biases, disaffections, and tempers. If you prefer putting a lot of effort into a sigil, wishing to create a "real piece of artwork," you are, of course, perfectly free to do so. It is recommended, however, for reasons to be discussed at greater length later, that you should not spend too much time *consciously* creating a sigil. This is because, among other arguments, it will be much more difficult to forget the sigil's outline and contents or to push it out of the consciousness, which is so essential for its proper working.

Before we start our discussion of the techniques for activating sigils, I would like to give you a few more practical tips.

The first recommendation involves the method of *constructing a sentence of desire.* Sigil magic is primarily success magic. It aims at achieving very tangible and verifiable results. Accordingly, sentences of will should be concrete and specific. Ambiguity will confuse the unconscious and may lead to only partial success at best, but more frequently it will provoke total failure.

My own experience has shown, as mentioned in chapter 1, that it is advisable to begin each sentence of desire with the same formula; in our example it was "THIS MY WISH... ." One might also simply say "I WISH..." or "IT IS MY WILL...," or something similar. Specifically mentioning the will is advantageous since the injunction given to the unconscious is clearer and easier to understand. Feeble phrasings such as "I WOULD LIKE TO...," "I WOULD WISH TO..." or "I SHOULD WANT TO..." lack conviction and should be avoided. In the end, you will always have to learn from your own experiences and find *your own* optimal formula.

We know from various other systems of manipulation of consciousness that negative formulas are usually not properly comprehended by the unconscious. While the unconscious is capable of understanding the metaphorical language (and sigils constructed with the word method are really nothing else) in expressions like "eradicate," "remove," or "avoid," it seems to ignore words like "not," "none," "never," etc., for most people. Therefore, do not say "THIS MY WISH *NOT* TO BECOME ILL," but say "THIS MY WISH TO REMAIN HEALTHY."

Interestingly enough, this does not apply to all areas of practical magic. For example, the difference between talismans and amulets is commonly defined in that talismans are *for* something while amulets are *against* something. Thus, a talisman may be constructed *for health;* however, an amulet would be constructed *against illness.* But even with amulets one will usually refrain from using negative formulations (e.g., "PROTECT ME FROM ALL ILLNESS," or something similar).

Later on, when we look at the theories which purport to explain how sigil magic works, we will realize that this mechanism has less to do with negative wording than with the general problem of how to get around the "psychic censor." The experiences of some magicians who have achieved success with negative formulas have confirmed this point of view. But this is an exception to the rule, and you should try to avoid any risk, especially when starting with your practical work.

The question as to whether one should formulate precisely or a bit "hazily" is arguable. In my experience, it is not sensible to dictate overly detailed directives to the unconscious. Sentences like "THIS MY WISH TO MEET FRANZ BARDON ON THE 17TH OF OCTOBER AT 3:32 P.M. IN SHARKY'S BAR" not only make great demands on your own Magis (or, as Mesoamerican shamans would label it, on your "control of the nagual") but also presuppose a rather generous, good-willed unconscious. One should never put too great a strain on the universe. But this is a general problem in practical magic, and the sigil magician is not the only one compelled to tackle it, as it also applies to the ceremonial magician, the sorcerer, and the theurgist.

Experience shows that it is quite feasible to include the time factor in the sentence of desire. For example, "THIS MY WISH TO BECOME HEALTHY AGAIN *THIS MONTH*," etc. But an overloaded psychic time schedule in manager fashion would definitely be too much for our magical faculty. In the chapter "But How Does It Work?" we will take a closer look at time factors and control of success.

Thus, you should try for a proper balance between wishy-washy and overly specific formulations. A sentence of desire of the "THIS MY WISH TO BE RATHER WELL" format is somewhat too vague, for even if the sigil did produce the desired success, you probably would not become aware of it. Spells for winning in a lottery in which you strive to fix the exact amount of money to the third decimal place will, due to information overload, force your whole system to collapse. At best, nothing will happen at all; at worst, however, the bailiff might suddenly turn up with a writ and his/her calculator. But, here again, personal experience is better than a thousand cookbooks.

Incidentally, it is advisable (at least sometimes), when using all the methods of sigil construction discussed here, for you to place a border round the sigil, either in the form of a triangle, circle, square, or something similar. See Figures 4, 5, and 6.

This has two advantages. First, it makes it easier to concentrate on the sigil when charging it. Second, it gives the sigil a "definite" and "conclusive" touch, for if you work a lot with sigils, occasionally you may find the sigils becoming "entangled" in your unconscious to form unde-

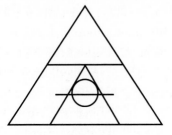

Figure 4

Figure 5

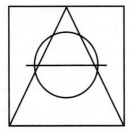

Figure 6

sirable chains and combinations. However, this happens very rarely, and the risk is comparatively small. It also happens mainly to sigil fanatics who don't do anything else all day long but inoculate their unconscious, cramming it full with glyphs. The sigil of Figure 3, however, is an example of a construction which does not need an additional border.

Another aspect of putting a border around the sigil is that Mandala structures (as depth pychology has shown) will awaken and activate archetypal material in the unconscious. Thus, a border will facilitate the arousal of the inner psychic elemental forces (Magis). If we look at the subject in greater depth, Mandalas (cf. Tibetan Thangkas and Yantras) are basically somewhat more complicated sigils that transport philosophical, mythical, spiritual, and similar contents, which, of course, can be said of most spiritual symbols anyway.

Before beginning our discussion of sigil activation, we shall take a closer look at how to simplify them. Overly complicated sigils are as ineffective as baroque tapeworm sentences of desire. Always keep in mind that you will have to internalize ("charge") the sigil in a state of magical or "gnostic" trance. This may mean that you will have to imagine it actively. Such a procedure might not be a problem as long as you actually have the sigil in front of you, such as hanging it on a wall or painting it onto a mirror, but even then it could be difficult to internalize a glyph with too many details to it. There are no limits to your fantasy or artistic talent when simplifying or stylizing sigils. You may even "cheat" a bit, as long as you are *emotionally satisfied with the result of your drawing.*

Let us look at a new example. The sentence of desire "THIS IS MY WISH TO EARN FIVE HUNDRED POUNDS TOMORROW" leaves us with the following letters:

T, H, I, ,S, M, Y, W, O, E, A, R, N, F, V, U, D, P

This long list of letters can form this general sigil:

Figure 7

Since this is far too complicated, we will want to simplify it:

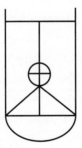

Figure 8

You will note that we have left out quite a lot, but we
have also added some embroideries or supplements, e.g.,
the vertical line drawn through the middle of the whole
sigil and the horizontal line cutting the whole circle in
half. What is important—at least in the beginning—is that
we *are theoretically able to rediscover all our basic letters in the
sigil (even in its stylized version).* Now we certainly won't

find it difficult to recognize the letters T, H, I, Y, W, O, E, V, U, D, and P, especially if we keep in mind that the same lines may be interpreted in several different fashions. The arc, for example, may stand at the same time for a U as well as for a D.

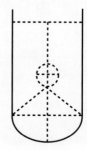

Figure 9

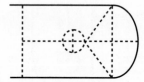

Figure 10

But what has happened to the letters S, R and M? And where is the A? If we want to keep the basic form of this sigil as it is, we will have to "cheat" a bit:

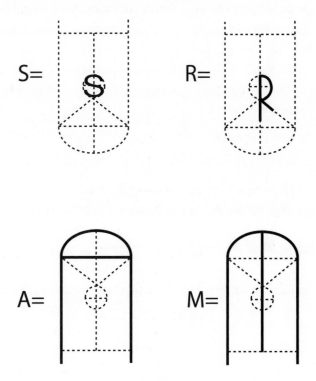

Figure 11

Admittedly, M and S might look a bit better, but, after all, we merely want to illustrate how to proceed with abstractions.

Now, it may be argued that nearly any letter could be rediscovered in nearly any glyph with this method, if you only had enough cheek and a vivid imagination. To some extent, this is certainly true, but the main point is that you are constructing the sigils so that all other possibilities become irrelevant.

THE PROCESS OF SIGIL CONSTRUCTION ITSELF IS MORE IMPORTANT THAN ITS GRAPHIC RESULT!

Of course, we do need the finished sigil, i.e., the graphic end result, for otherwise we could not charge or activate it. But it would be of no use to you at all if you had not constructed it alone, without any outside help. (We will discuss some exceptions to this rule in our chapter on the pictorial method.) The above mentioned mnemonic is little more than a rephrasing of an exhortation which you will hear frequently from Zen masters—"The way is the goal...."

Perhaps we should now deal with how to decorate a sigil. We have already seen that it is important that the sigil strikes us as being "magical," "out of the ordinary." This will mean different things to different people. My own style of sigil construction, which I have developed in the course of more than 12 years of practice, prefers horizontal glyphs with squiggles and triangles for decoration. So I would decorate the sigil from the last example in this fashion (Figure 12):

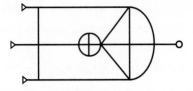

Figure 12

These embroideries do not have a meaning in themselves (just as a sigil no longer has any consciously "recognizable" meaning); they serve the sole purpose of creating the right "atmosphere" or giving the sigil a "magic" touch (or, for the more romantically minded, a touch of "mystery"). This can enhance its effect substantially, and I strongly advise you to experiment.

Chapter 3

The Magical Trance/ Activating the Sigil

The following can be applied equally to the word and the pictorial method. Within limits, the various techniques are pertinent to the mantrical spell method as well, but this mode shall be explained separately in more detail in a later chapter.

Recommendation for a lightning-charging
(for people who are always in a hurry)

Having finished the sigil with much effort, go to bed with it. Masturbate and, during sexual climax, concentrate on the graphic sigil. If you have a well-trained imagination, you might as well visualize the sigil, but beginners are advised to stare at the glyph with widely opened eyes. It is crucial that you place the sigil in front of your eyes *during orgasm.*

DO *NOT* THINK OF YOUR SENTENCE OF DESIRE OR THE CONTENTS OF YOUR SIGIL AT THIS MOMENT!

Ideally, you should have forgotten the original purpose for which the sigil was created. (To achieve this, you can put the sigil aside for a couple of days or weeks after construction and then take it out in a quiet minute to activate it. But this, of course, could hardly be termed a "lightning ritual.")

Afterwards, you will have to *banish the sigil.* The best method of banishing is roaring laughter. It does not matter if this may seem a bit artificial; if you can think of a good joke now, even better. Immediately after banishing by laughter, *think of something completely different.* The easiest way of achieving this is by switching on the TV, listening to the latest lottery results, jumping up and down on one leg for half an hour, etc.

One may argue endlessly about sexual ethics and / or sexual fears, but it is an undeniable fact that sigils are best internalized in the easiest, speediest, and least problematical way during sexual climax. We will get to know various other methods, too, but experience has shown that orgasm provides the most effective of magical trances. Debauchees with glittering eyes may, however, be warned that this branch of sexual magic has little or nothing to do with sexual "fun." In the past, when it was still trendy to work with "sacrifices" of all sorts, it was common to speak of "sacrificing the orgasmic lust on the altar of Transcendence," etc. Obviously, this has a lot to do with Tantric and Taoist ideas, which state that the male should at all costs avoid the explosive orgasm (i.e., ejaculation) during sacred sexual intercourse because, according to these doctrines, loss of semen means loss of power (and, by extrapolation, longevity). This approach, which has for various reasons never become particularly popular in the West, led even one of the major masters of sexual magic, Aleister Crowley, to concentrate on drinking his sperm after sexual intercourse (in heterosexual intercourse, the mixed male and female secretions—Crowley's infamous "elixir"). This digression aside, we may note that lecherous sex maniacs won't have too much pleasure when dealing with this branch of sexual magic, as these operations can be rather strenuous and not too pleasurable.

In the first chapter it was mentioned that sigils should be internalized *spasmodically*. This can be done in several ways. Our goal is always the same: to form an altered state of consciousness in which the practitioner has become "soft" and in which s/he will no longer or cannot prevent direct communication between the conscious and the unconscious. Like the magical or gnostic trance in general, consciousness is not entirely switched off, which means that you aren't aiming for a hypnotic full trance. Such "threshold states"[11] may be achieved either by withholding sleep, by overexertion, by exhaustion, or by activating intense emotions like anger, fear, pleasure, ecstasy, etc.[12] Here again we can see why the sex-magical charging of a sigil (which, of course, can also be performed during intercourse with a partner) is so much easier than all other methods. First, most people are quite familiar with willed orgasms, which can hardly be said, for example, of willed, controlled trances of exhaustion or horror. Second, the effort to achieve a sexual climax is so much less than to achieve a trance through fasting, for another example, which would take several days of starving oneself, or a fear trance, for which you might have to hang half of your body out of the window on the seventeenth floor of a building. (Of course, a high ride on a roller coaster might do the trick as well, but can you really control your acrophobia enough to charge a sigil?) Nevertheless, you should get to know as many different circumstances for sigil charging as possible to widen your scope of magical techniques considerably.

One technique which is frequently quoted in literature, but hardly ever explained in detail, is Spare's so-called *death posture.* Whereas Pete Carroll in *Liber Null* (p. 31), following on from other writers, basically sees it as a method of "holding one's breath in an uncomfortable position until one nearly dies," Kenneth Grant[13] regards it as belonging to sex magic. He sees the death posture (referring to Spare himself) as a technique whereby the conscious mind is switched off (that is to say, "intermediately slain") by sexual activity, which means that all conscious thoughts will cease. Anyway, the crucial point, as with most magical trances, is that you can achieve a state of non-thinking or no-mind in this way, whereby the conscious mind collapses for a short span of time (sometimes, as with an orgasm, only for seconds) and leaves free a direct channel to the unconscious. In the following text, two non-sexual variants of the death posture, which have proved themselves well in practice, particularly for people who are new to magic and who have little or no training in magical trances, are described.

Death Posture (Version 1)

This version may be performed both in a standing or a sitting position. For your first attempts, I recommend sitting before a table on which you have placed the sigil.

After a deep breath, block your eyes, ears, mouth and nose, using the fingers of both hands. Concentrate on the internal tension in your body (do *not* think of the sigil or its aim!), and hold your breath until you truly cannot bear it any longer. Then, shortly before reaching the point of fainting, open wide your eyes and stare—while breathing in and out fresh air—at the sigil. If you do this correctly, you will find yourself in a state of almost panic-stricken no-mind—a form of magical trance where your unconscious is more responsive to and more receptive of sigils. Afterwards, as already mentioned, you banish by laughter and by concentrating on something completely different, the more secular the better.

One version of this technique has already been described in chapter 1. It is performed by standing in front of a mirror on which you have drawn your sigil with water-soluble colors. Here again, physical overexertion is employed. Stare into the eyes of your mirror image without fluttering your eyelids, then cross your arms behind your head or your neck, push your arms backwards as far and uncomfortably as you can, and tense all your muscles while holding your breath (you may also stand on tiptoes). Keep this posture until you cannot bear the tension and/or pain anymore. Then release the tension spasmodically while internalizing the sigil. Banish by laughter, think of something else, etc.

A *note of caution:*

Version 1 of the death posture is NOT suitable for persons who suffer from heart condition, ailments of the lung, or high blood pressure. Since you can hardly ask your doctor whether s/he would advise you against this technique or not (unless the doctor is also a magician—you might already have found one by using a sigil!), you should, if in doubt, choose one of the other aforementioned techniques.

Death Posture (Version 2)

As far as I know, this technique has never before been described in writing. It is "milder" than the first version but easily as effective, although it demands a little bit of training. It is performed in a sitting position.

The sigil lies in front of you on the table. You sit in a chair as straight as you can, your palms resting on the table. You may extend your thumbs and let them touch each other, the sigil now lying in the open square of your hands. Stare at the sigil without blinking your eyelids. It does not matter if your eyes start watering; your attention is concentrated elsewhere. Now try to twitch the muscles of your calves *very briefly.* It is best to start with one leg, then to change to the other, and finally to twitch the muscles of both calves together. The twitching itself should be tense but at the same time loose. A split second is quite enough as long as it is very intense. This may sound a bit difficult at first, but with a little practice you will know precisely what is right for you.

Now you may continue by twitching the muscles of your upper arms, following with your chest, hands, and arms, up to your scalp (which may be a purely subjective feeling, but having experienced it once you will know how to do it properly). With a little practice, the whole procedure should not last longer than about half a second. So, your entire body is racked by a short spasm, and at the climax you open your eyes even more widely (while still staring at the sigil), "inhale the sigil" with your eyes, laugh loudly while closing your eyes, and that's it! (Then, once again think of something completely different, etc.)

Don't despair if you should encounter some minor problems in the beginning. Your organism is only as human as you are, but with a little bit of effort you will master this technique in the true meaning of the word: lightning-fast. Also, you will have a method of sigil activation in hand which works even faster than the sex-magical one! I have seen workshop participants who managed to get the effect of the sigil minutes after their first attempt, and this is quite common.

Note: After charging a sigil, you should avoid meditation and all other trance-inducing techniques (e.g., trance dance, drugs, brain machines, etc.) for at least three hours. As you have firmly "shut the lid" of your unconscious by banishing and distraction, it is advisable to let it rest for a while to forgo the possibility of the sigils floating into your consciousness again.

THE FASTER YOU FORGET THE SIGIL,
THE MORE EFFECTIVE THE OPERATION.

As with talismans, amulets, and magical rituals in general, the intent to forget a desire or magical operation is one of the greatest tasks for a magician if s/he wants to experience success quickly. Experience with meditation and thought control will certainly pay off now. You may have heard the story of the man who came to his guru and asked him what to do to become enlightened. "Nothing," the guru answered. "Just go on living as you did before. Oh, yes, there is one thing, though: avoid thinking of the monkey." Very pleased, the man thanked his guru and returned home. But while on his way home, his thoughts began circling remorselessly: "I must not think of the monkey, I must not think of the monkey ..."[14]

Why forgetting a sigil is of such prime importance in this form of magic will be illustrated later when we take a look at possible explanation models for this magical method. After having activated/internalized a sigil, you should not think of the glyph itself nor of its content. Since most people have a rather bad memory for complicated symbols and glyphs (painters, graphic artists, and others who are particularly visually gifted or working in this field excepted), forgetting the sigil itself won't present too much of a problem, unless the glyph's design is too simple. (To forget a square or triangle could prove rather difficult.)

Forget the contents of the sigil and the sentence of desire. If sigils or sentences of desire unexpectedly pop up into consciousness, recharge and banish them again. Most of the time it's enough to simply distract your attention from the "monkey" by laughter, for example (which, as pointed out several times in *Liber Null,* is one of the best techniques of exorcism anyway).

You should definitely keep a diary for your sigil work, if only to check on your successes at a later date, but you should also conceal the sigils, sentences of desire, and other details (e.g., by placing a sheet of paper over the relevant sections) so that they won't come back into your memory accidentally when you open your diary or leaf through it. As with the formulation of the sentence of desire, you will have to find a compromise between permanent memory and complete loss of any documentation.

As to awaiting the success of the operation, *don't do it!* This is also the best way of making sure that you will forget about it. If this is too extreme for you and if you have problems with forgetting, try to counter this with that state of consciousness which Spare termed the "Neither/Neither." Ray Sherwin tags it "Nonattachment/Nondisinterest," or, more precisely, "positive Non-desire."[15] This again is more a question of practice and self-discipline than of technique.

There is yet one other technique for forgetting a sigil, namely getting used to it until you no longer perceive it consciously. You may be familiar with this principle from personal experience. You decide to do something special every day and, therefore, you hang a note in a prominent place as a reminder. For a few days this will work all right until you get so accustomed to the note that it does not serve as a reminder, so you finally end up where you began. You just don't see the note and its message anymore. This may even become an unconscious act of sigil magic achieving the desired success. More likely, however, the whole procedure was nothing but well-intentioned amateur work. Now we may use the same technique with sigils by employing this very pattern of behavior or perception. After charging the sigil, you place it in a prominent position until you are no longer consciously aware of it. As mentioned previously, you may also engrave the glyph on the outer side of a ring or into a metal plate as a talisman, etc.

Sigils and Talismans/Amulets

Basically, it is of no importance at all which material you use to draw your final sigil on before it is charged. If you are a traditionalist-purist and want to use virgin parchment, you may do so, of course, but normal paper is quite good enough.[16] After activation, sigils are usually burned or otherwise destroyed, but you can also make talismans and amulets out of them. In this case, you will want to use more durable materials.

One way of doing this is by drawing the sigil on a piece of parchment or sturdy paper. If you charge it sex magically, you may put some sexual secretions (or blood or saliva) on it for support after activation. After banishing, you can roll up the paper or parchment and wrap some yarn or silk thread around it. Depending upon which school of "isolation techniques" you belong to, you may either seal this roll with pure beeswax or sew it into a piece of silk, linen or leather, etc. If you want to wear the amulet or talisman, it is advisable to make it into a necklace or tie it to a thong. Having served its purpose, the magical tool has to be burned, buried or thrown in water. Before doing so, you can discharge it under running water with a suitable suggestion.

As pointed out in the beginning, the advantage of Spare's sigil magic is that it has no need for complicated rituals. Neither do you need to engage in calculating specific astrological constellations, cabbalistic arithmetic or lunar phases, etc. You will be better off, especially when practicing Pragmatic Magic, if you have at hand at least *one* of these systems that can be performed without such complicated and time-consuming considerations, as useful as they may be at other times. This will keep you on the ball, ready for action and versatile.

You don't really need amulets and talismans in sigil magic, either. If the sigil is charged correctly, you already have created an "astral talisman" (or "astral amulet") of sorts, a new circuit in the psycho-computer which will remain effective until it has served its purpose. Such a magical weapon has the advantage of being independent of physical objects (which also means that it can never get into the wrong hands). It is usually those "magicians" with the least practical experience who shout the loudest that a "correctly protected" magical weapon never would get into the wrong hands in the first place. Unfortunately, this is not necessarily the case.

Every beginner in ceremonial magic learns that his/her rituals will attract astral entities just as light will attract moths. With magical weapons, talismans, amulets and other appropriate tools, the case is quite similar: some people are fascinated by them beyond sensible control. It is of little use to warn people never to touch the magically charged tools of a sorcerer without his/her permission, for proscriptions will usually make the whole thing seem a lot more attractive. It is of far lesser importance that a magician may have to do without his/her talisman, for example, after having been robbed of it. The whole situation can be compared with the position of an Army Quartermaster: he is responsible for the safekeeping of his arms and ammunition, not so much because any loss of gear would weaken his arsenal (which, of course, is another aspect not to be ignored), but mainly to ensure the safety of others who may not be aware of the danger of such tools—and who might have to pay dearly with their lives or physical or psychic health for their ignorance or innocence. It is no secret either that some magical instruments do tend to develop a definite, independent life of their own, and the history of magic is full of examples to prove the point.

When using non-physical sigils, you don't have to make tiresome last provisions concerning what should be done about them after your death so that they will be properly deactivated or handed over to the proper magical heir, etc. While sigils might show up again in your consciousness sometimes, this is quite harmless. I have never observed sigils developing a totally independent existence, going off on their own, etc., like amulets, magical daggers, and the like are sometimes wont to do.

Now, what about controlling your own success? Basically, the same rules are applicable here as in more conventional magic. Sigil magic is certainly not an infallible technique, but numerous practitioners have confirmed repeatedly that it is by far the most effective of all the Western magical systems. If your sigil working has a time limit (for example, one month, a quarter of a year, etc.), control of success is simple enough. You may make a special note in your diary's agenda and later contemplate the result. Things are a bit more complicated if there are no time limits or the objective is an extremely long-term one. Nevertheless, with some practice you will develop the right feeling for it. Although you will have long forgotten your sigil working, the moment you realize your success, you will remember, which may create quite a weird feeling at times. You might have a similar experience as the Hasidic rabbi when he thanked God for never sending him anything before he needed it! It is a prerogative that we accustom ourselves to a different manner of success assessment.

The time it takes for a sigil to work is somewhat unpredictable. Sometimes success will be instant; sometimes it may take months. We are told that Austin Osman Spare could bring forth a cloudburst within minutes with the aid of sigils. He also succeeded, using this method, in evoking demons at a flinch. Nevertheless, it would be presumptuous to ascribe this to sigil magic and its techniques alone. Certainly, the magician's personal talent, the power of his/her own Magis, the inner consistency of his/her magical universe, the qualities of magical time (which shamans label "moments of power"), and some degree of probability may play an important part in instant magical phenomena, which should not be underestimated. But this is, as I have pointed out before, not a problem of sigil magic alone. As did Dion Fortune, I tend to operate on a time limit of about six to nine months in general. If short-term or medium-term operations have not succeeded within this period, they should be considered as having failed. You will find more tips for the practical use of sigils in chapter 8.

For didactic reasons I chose to start off with the word method of sigilization to escort you to practical work immediately, without initially giving any consideration to other methods of sigil construction. In doing so, we avoided overburdening you with technicalities at too early a stage, parts of which you would only understand through practice anyway. Another reason is that most readers will probably want to start off with the word method because it is the most simple and uncomplicated one. The other methods of sigil construction follow. Points which have already been discussed and which are also applicable for these types of sigils will not be repeated, but, of course, I shall clarify distinctions in procedure.

Chapter 4

The Pictorial Method

As opposed to the word method and the mantrical spell method, the pictorial method of sigil construction demands neither language nor specifically formulated sentences of desire. Its advantage lies in the fact that you are able to use the image language of the unconscious directly, provided that you are able to transcribe precisely your sentence of desire into such images without utilizing words.

Imagine that you want to heal a friend. Let us assume his name is Hank Miller and that he is suffering from stomach pains. Similarly to Voodoo doll magic, you might draw a figure with his initials (see Figure 13).

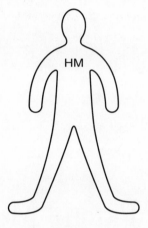

Figure 13

Then you may stick an "astral acupuncture needle" into his stomach area through which healing energy is fed into the affected part of the body (Figure 14):

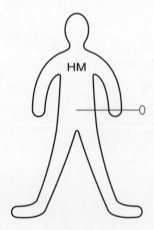

Figure 14

This sigil must now be simplified and stylized as with the word method. See Figures 15 and 16.

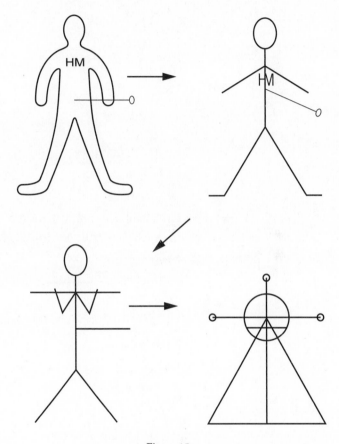

Figure 15

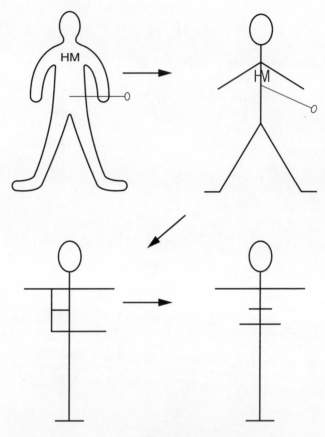

Figure 16

Charging or activating/internalizing is executed as already described in chapters 1 and 3. The same rules are
applicable for forgetting the operation, etc.

Let us look at a second example. Two people (part-
ners) are to be brought together by a so-called "binding
spell." We'll call them "A" and "B." See Figure 17.

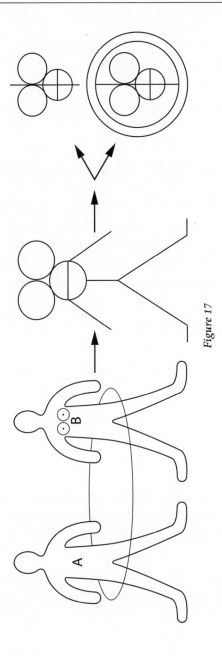

Figure 17

If you work a lot with the pictorial method, you will find that soon you will want to develop your own "symbolic language" in order to tackle more complicated subjects. This leads us into the realm of the Alphabet of Desire, covered in chapter 6. If you are familiar with magical symbols in general, you may use them as "raw material" for individual sigils as well. This, of course, requires that these glyphs and signs have truly become second nature to you. Let us again look at an example to illustrate this procedure. We want to create a familiar spirit or "psychogone" and will, therefore, need such basic symbols. Thus, we must choose from the rich treasury of our history of occult symbols. Let us assume that the spirit: a) should be hard working; b) should have structural awareness and the ability to materialize itself; and c) it must furnish you with financial advantages. We want to utilize the symbols of Earth and Saturn. See Figure 18.

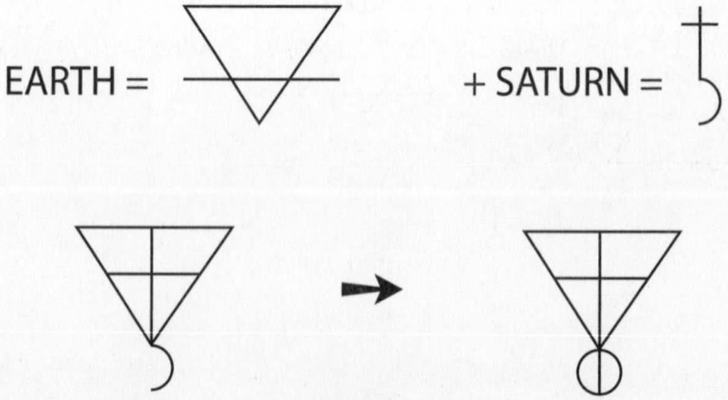

Figure 18

We may also want to create a spirit from the sphere of Venus for erotic purposes. To this end, we might use the symbols in Figure 19.

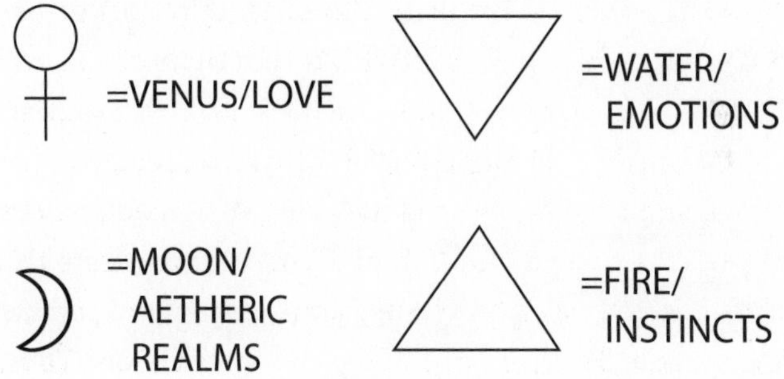

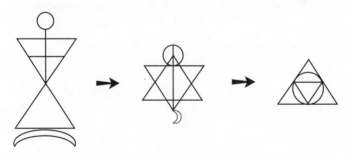

♀ =VENUS/LOVE   ▽ =WATER/ EMOTIONS

☽ =MOON/ AETHERIC REALMS   △ =FIRE/ INSTINCTS

Figure 19

Combined, these symbols may form one of the sigils in Figure 20.

Figure 20

The following symbols may be used to form a sigil for achieving mystical insight into infinity:

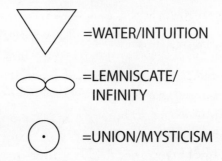

=WATER/INTUITION

=LEMNISCATE/
 INFINITY

=UNION/MYSTICISM

See Figure 21 for completed sigils.

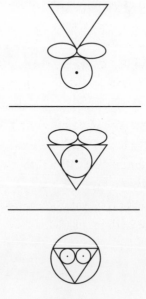

Figure 21

Of course, you may also use Hebrew letters, *tattwa* symbols, or any geometrical symbols you prefer. (There are very few glyphs which have not been attributed with some meaning.) But as pointed out before, you should not just copy some symbols out of books which have no life for you or are not vivid to you. Naturally, you may live in the paradigm that these "ancient" symbols have already developed a life of their own, having been vitalized by legions of magicians before us, but even in that case you will first have to create an inner contact to the glyphs yourself, e.g., by employing them frequently in a pertinent magical context.

One could object that this technique contradicts the basis of Spare's system because it does not work with individual sigils. However, this is only partly correct. The individual elements making up such a sigil may consist of established symbols, but the end result is definitely individual because of the selection of the basic symbols and the simplification/stylization and decoration, which is executed here again. The sigils from our last examples could be enlarged in the manner of Figure 22.

Let us not forget that alienation is a significant element of sigil construction.

Now that we have covered the important aspects of the pictorial method, let us take a look at the mantrical spell method.

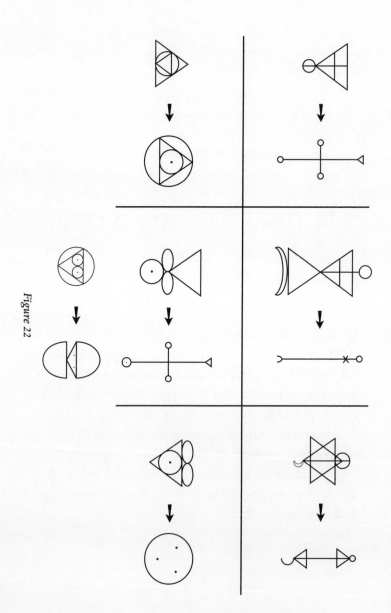

Figure 22

Chapter 5

The Mantrical Spell Method

The *mantrical spell method* basically employs *acoustic* sigils. The principle of constructing mantrical sigils is quite simple: the sentence of desire is transformed into a mantra devoid of any obvious sense or meaning. This may be done most easily by writing down the sentence of desire in a quasi-phonetic manner, i.e., words as spoken. This may demand some ingenuity, but any magician needs this, and, here again, practice alone makes for refinement. Let us take an example from *Liber Null* (p. 21):

a) Sentence of desire:
I WANT TO MEET A SUCCUBUS IN DREAM

This sentence, in a quasi-phonetic (acoustic) spelling, becomes:

b) I WAH NAR MEDAR SUKU BUSIN DREEM

c) Now, all double or multiple letters are eliminated, as with the word method:

I WAH NAR MEDAR
SUKU BUSIN DREEM

d) This leaves us with:[17]
    IWAH N'MER D'SUK

e) The sentence from d) is now rearranged, or alien-ated even more, and you are free to add some vowels so that the end product does not become a tongue twister but can be easily vocalized:

HAWI EMNER KUSAD (completed mantra)

For the use of mantrical sigils, you will need some linguistic agility and an ear for rhythm. The sigil mantras should sound euphonic (meaning "nice") as well as "some-how magical." At the same time, they should be alienated enough so that you won't be able to recognize the original sentence of desire.

Activating/Internalization of Mantrical Sigils

Unlike word or pictorial sigils, sigil mantras are usually not activated/internalized spasmodically ("short and in-tense"); instead, they are repeated rhythmically and mo-notonously. An exception to this rule are the "words of power," which are sometimes sigilized, as we shall see later on.

In Eastern cultures mantras are also employed to induce magical trances and mystical states of consciousness, etc., because they tend to tranquilize the conscious mind when monotonously repeated over a long period of time. Thus, the psychic censor is softened up and direct access to the unconscious is granted. Naturally, mantras play a very important part in Mantra-Yoga, Tantra (of Hindu and Buddhist origin), Buddhism (including Zen!), and many other Eastern philosophies. These mantras may be more or less free of recognizable sense (for example, "HRAM HRIM HRUM"), or they may carry a meaning (for example, "OM MANI PEME HUM," which, as you may know, approximates "HAIL TO THEE, JEWEL IN THE LOTUS BLOSSOM"). They may express a certain form of worship and heightening of awareness. Islam (especially Sufism) knows its mantras, as does Catholicism, which uses them, for example, in its rosary litanies, and shamans all over the world are known to work with different forms of mantras.

While a sound knowledge of mantra theory can be of help when using mantrical sigils, it is not strictly necessary. Sometimes it may even prove to be an outright obstacle if you are for some reason (e.g., conditioning, dogma, etc.) incapable of working with any but one special, established system.

Our sentence of desire has been turned into a mantra by manipulating its sound elements until we cannot recognize its meaning anymore (as is also the case with word and pictorial sigils). You can now activate this acoustic sigil by repeating it over and over again, for hours on end, if possible. The monotony of this procedure will guide you into a kind of "mantra-stupor" (this will follow naturally and may sometimes occur even after only a few minutes chanting); thus, your directive for the unconscious, which is now concealed in the acoustic sigil, can pass the censor to thrive in the depths of the psyche and go about its work. You may support this procedure by a trance of exhaustion, achieved, for example, by fasting, prolonged lack of sleep, or extreme physical exertion. You might even use autohypnosis by playing the mantra on repeat with an audio device during your sleep, but experience has shown that this is not really requisite except as an auxiliary measure.

After charging the mantra, banish by laughter and immediately distract the conscious mind as described in chapter 3.

Words of Power

Instead of fashioning lengthy sigil mantras, a single "Word of Power" may be formed using the same construction technique as described above. Let us take the example of the aforementioned succubus evocation. The finished mantra in the end was:

HAWI EMNER KUSAD

We might take the first syllable from each word and construct a new word:

HA EM KU = HAEMKU

We could also take the last syllable of each word:

WI NER SAD = WINERSAD

Other possible combinations in this example are:

WINERKU, HANERSAD, KUNERWI, SADEMHA, etc.

You will realize that the possibilities offered by this technique are practically unlimited.

Activating/Internalizing Words of Power

When charging, you may proceed as you would with longer sigil mantras: by chanting it monotonously for a long time.

Or, you may proceed spasmodically as with the word or pictorial method, using the techniques described in chapter 3. Instead of an optical internalization, you perform an acoustic one: at the peak of the tension (regardless of whether you use sex-magical techniques or the various versions of the death posture) you shout aloud the word of power—the louder the better, because this drives away all disturbing thoughts and even interrupts the entire ability to think for the duration of the exclamation. Here again, don't forget to banish the operation by laughter and then distract your attention. The technique of the infamous "death cry" of the Australian aborigines is based on a very similar principle.

The only disadvantage of the mantrical spell method is that it is not particularly silent. Therefore, usually you will have to be alone when using it, unless you are lucky enough to live with people who are in sympathy with your magical "quirks," or are completely deaf. Anyone familiar with mantra systems will be aware of the fact that there are generally three stages of mantra intonation (the so-called "JapaMantra"): loud, low, and silent (or mental) intonation. The mental intonation is considered to be the "highest" form of mantra working and is quite complicated. These hints, however, should enable you to experiment with quite a number of different mantra techniques.

Incidentally, it seems more than likely that some of the medieval spells were constructed in the same, or at least in a very similar, manner. Albeit most of the handed-down formulas are little else than mutilated church Latin or Hebrew, and even though most of the other spells have almost certainly been constructed via cabbalistic gematria or have been received as a "revelation" of sorts, there are a number of formulas and "barbarous names of evocation" which cannot be explained as such etymologically. However, this has to remain pure speculation for the time being.

It will largely depend on your own temperament and on your predilections whether you use the word, pictorial, or mantrical spell method. Whereas I myself favor the word method and, occasionally, the pictorial method, I must admit that the mantrical spell method has borne the most amazing and speediest results. Perhaps this is precisely so because I personally do not like it very much! Thus, it is certainly advisable to experiment with all three methods. The sigil's energy quality or the way the sigil "feels" is completely different from method to method. After a short time, you will know exactly which method is most promising for any given operation. Being a true magician, you will not tolerate one-sidedness because you know that in the course of your magical career you will be challenged too often and will be confronted with the most varied of problems. It is always beneficial to keep one's arsenal of possibilities and weapons in good shape as well as to stay in practice with "remote" techniques.

The ultimate sigil is surely silence itself, but of this nothing can be said. For "the Tao that can be described is not the Divine Tao."

Chapter 6

The Alphabet of Desire

We will now discuss one of the most fascinating chapters of Spare's sigil magic, the Alphabet of Desire. It is also one of the more complicated and least explored areas, not the least reason for this being the desolate situation of literary sources. Spare's writings per se are very ambiguous and difficult to follow, and his exposition of the Alphabet of Desire is no exception. Even concerning his original comments we can only rely on Kenneth Grant,[18] who seems intent on concealing more than he wants to divulge.

Apparently, Spare conceived the Alphabet of Desire as a system of 22 glyphs, all of them expressing, to use his own words, "aspects of sexuality." In none of his writings published to date do we find all of these "letters" fully listed, let alone explained. Nevertheless, we do have a number of clues as to what Spare meant by them. In general, Grant seems to stick quite strictly to the original and gives us many enlightening insights. Pete Carroll's account in *Liber Null* (pages 76–87) does not necessarily have a lot in common with Spare's original system (a fact which was pointed out to me—somewhat indignantly—by Frater ∴ Thanatos of the O.T.O.), but, as I see it, Carroll is on the right track. To date, the German author Markus Jungkurth[19] has been the only writer who deals with Spare's alphabet in more detail. But while he does quote the odd word or two from Spare's own writings by way of explanation, he gives us very few clues for actual practice, unfortunately.

Spare's statement that the Alphabet of Desire is part of a special proto-language of man's (or possibly actually Spare's) own unconscious does, however, give us an important practical clue, particularly if we are familiar with the techniques involved in construing artificial ritual languages.[20] It would be wrong to assume that Spare, who as a magician was an absolute pragmatist, understood it as being a universal and categorical proto-alphabet for use by all people. This would contradict his entire system, and we do not have a single convincing indication why we should take this for granted. The following explanations should, therefore, be understood as my own, personal interpretations. The approach described hereafter has proven to be effective enough in my practical work, and we can find similar methods in other systems as well,[21] but we must admit that we are more or less breaking virgin soil here. The advantage of this approach is that it leaves enough room for personal exploration, which might especially appeal to the more experienced sigil magician.

Basically, I shall describe two main forms of approach and ways of dealing with the alphabet in this chapter: 1) the Alphabet of Desire as a principle of structure embedded in a framework; and 2) the Alphabet of Desire as a mirror of the psyche created by chains of associations. Although some overlap may occur occasionally, one should not forget that these are truly two entirely different approaches.

The Alphabet of Desire as a Structuring Principle

Pete Carroll has presented us, in his well-known laconic and precise manner, with this model in *Liber Null* (pp. 76–87). Unfolding his system, he does not base it—as did Spare—on purely sexual functions. Strictly speaking, his system is more of an "Alphabet of Emotions." These emotions he arranges as "complementary dualisms": FRIGHT/ATTRACTION, JOY/TERROR, GREED/AVERSION, etc. Not all of these complementary dualisms will seem convincing at first glance. For example, it may not be absolutely clear to everybody why ATROPHY/FRUSTRATION and RELEASE/DISSOLUTION should be seen as supplementary *opposites,* and even his scant explanations do not help us a lot. Incidentally, he does not stick strictly to Spare's division of 22 either, so we are justified in viewing his system as being an original creation of his own, following the Spare tradition.

Carroll's matrix will not be explained in detail here, but rather we will use it as an illustration to demonstrate by this *one* example how anyone can create his/her own Alphabet of Desire. Carroll divides his emotions in doublets: LUST/DESTRUCTION; DISSOLUTION/RELEASE; ATTACHMENT/LOATHING; RAPTURE/ANGER; GREED/AVERSION; ATTRACTION/FRIGHT; JOY/TERROR; ATROPHY/FRUSTRATION. Additionally, there are four categories which are, so to speak, "outside of competition": LAUGHTER, DECONCEPTUALIZATION, CONCEPTUALIZATION and UNION. And finally, he adds a "Supplementary Alphabet in Malkuth," which in his system covers the so-called "somatic emotions," namely PAIN/PLEASURE and DEPRESSION/ELATION.

But this is not the end of his system. The five meta-levels also play a significant role. The first three are based on alchemical symbolism, describing "the three states of matter" of each emotion: the Mercurial (☿), the Sulphurous (🜍), and the Earthy (🜁) levels. The Mercurial form indicates states of over-stimulation and dissolution of consciousness followed by catharsis or ecstasy (p. 76). The Sulphurous form indicates "the normal functional mode of the emotion," thus lying in between the Mercurial and Earthy mode, both of which derive from the first principle, comparable to the state of the "prima materia" in alchemy. The Earthy form is one of repression and unrealistic/unrealizable emotions.

The other two meta-structures are based on the principles of SOLVE ET COAGULA. The SOLVE principle (separation, repulsion, avoidance) includes the terms DEATH, HATE, FEAR, PAIN, and DEPRESSION. The COAGULA principle (attraction, coming together) comprises the terms SEX, LOVE, DESIRE, PLEASURE, and ELATION. The opposite pairs with which we have already dealt may be assigned to the above-mentioned generic terms. Thus, for example, LOVE (COAGULA level) includes emotions like ATTACHMENT, PASSION and RAPTURE, whereas their opposites (LOATHING, AGGRESSION and ANGER) belong to the category of HATE (SOLVE level), etc. This may appear rather complicated, and it probably is.

Finally, I should mention that all these emotions and principles have their own sigils or glyphs. For example:

DEATH (generic term) = ♄
DESTRUCTION
    (noncategory / emotion) = ⊗
SEX (generic term) = ☾
LUST (noncategory / emotion) = ♇

For further details, please refer to *Liber Null* itself.

The above notes should illustrate the structure of human emotions. Any number of other systems of order may be used and developed. For example, the four elements Earth, Water, Fire, and Air may be employed as major categories, as well as the ten sephiroth, the 22 paths of the cabbalistic Tree of Life (an approach may be found in *Liber Null*, pp. 77 and 86), the 12 energy qualities of the zodiac, Timothy Leary's and Robert Anton Wilson's circuits, etc. Since humankind has been attempting for thousands of years to understand itself, its environment, and life in general in structural terms ("God created the world according to measure and number"), it probably won't be all that easy to find one's *own,* truly original scheme of order which is entirely different from all former systems. At the same time, this gives us an insight into the basic structures of the human psyche, i.e., archetypal patterns which we should always implement in magic anyway. In other words, it does not really matter whether or not the pattern depends upon the structures of perception as influenced by the construction of the brain or hormones. What is important is the fact that we can find some of these patterns of order in all human beings and thus in every psyche. (Experts on ecclesiastical history will be pleased to remember in this context the good old nominalism squabblings of scholasticism; but then, it is a truism that our unresolved karma will always haunt us—even as a collective entity—to the umpteenth generation ...)

Let us take dualism, for example. Most people are familiar with polarized thinking and perception, independent of their cultural or civilizational background, of political, historical, economical, or social factors, etc. Even the ontological monism of many religions and philosophical systems is a convention of revolt against this polar / dual view, thus defining itself by denying it. It is of no consequence at all that most systems (including the purely magical ones, not to mention those of mysticism) look for a synthesis and dissolution of the polarities. This quest for the Grail is essentially a proof for the existence of dualism, at least when viewed as an ontological problem.

Now we understand that the Alphabet of Desire has developed into a significant instrument of the dawning of consciousness merely by having been created. If you want to construct your own alphabet following the structuring method described above, you will have to figure out those elements which you want to include and which can personify the energies of *your own psyche*. Just listing them is not good enough, however. You will have to find a proper framework for them.

Let us start with a modest example. For reasons of simplicity, we will experiment with the four elements EARTH, WATER, FIRE, and AIR. This is a system with which most magicians will be at least somewhat familiar. As a further framework we will choose DUALISM for the reasons mentioned. Looking for emotional and character qualities which form dualities, we assign them to the elements as follows (this, of course, is but one of many possible examples):

WATER

Love
Peaceableness
Need for Adaptation

FIRE

△

Hate
Aggression
Will to Conquest

EARTH

Pain
Striving for Stability
Perseverance

AIR

Joy
Impulse for change
Flexibility

Now I will discuss a sigil language, a canon of symbols, the particular use of which we will come to later. One possibility is to develop the chosen sigil, perhaps by applying the word method (whereby the chosen word itself serves as raw material) and combining it with the glyph of the major category. The four examples of Figure 23 clarify this process. You will observe that we are taking the basic symbol and combining it with the letters of the term.

Of course, these relationships are open to argument. For example, one could assign pain to the element of FIRE, which would imply a strong, nearly spastic feeling; pain within the element of EARTH would tend to be dull and lethargic, etc. One may also work with sub-elements such as EARTH OF WATER, AIR OF WATER, FIRE OF WATER, etc. Use your own intuition.

You may also utilize the pictorial method. LOVE, for example, might be (⏀) or (✚) (symbols of "union"), but these symbols might equally stand for SEX for the same reasons. This leads us a bit further into the area of philosophical and psychological cognition and evaluation. If, for example, you consider LOVE as an all-embracing principle (which need not necessarily be endorsed by everybody!), you could perhaps choose this sigil: (∞). HATE could then—for you—be its negation (for example: ⊗) or its dissolution (◯). For you, JOY might be the bundling of energies into ecstasy: (↑), or else it could be the blowing up or overcoming of fetters: (⟵╫⟶) or (⬌).

You will note that the construction of your own Alphabet of Desire demands not only a lot of thinking and intuition but great effort and hard work as well.

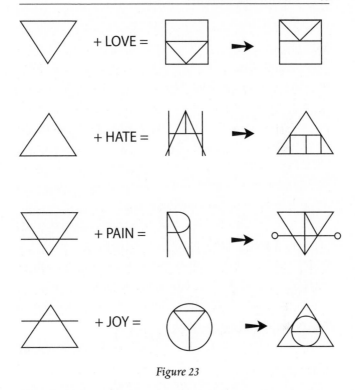

Figure 23

Let us now discuss the advantages and the possible applications of this sigil language before we tackle the second construction method of such an alphabet.

First of all, dealing with the Alphabet of Desire trains symbolic thinking and perception. This is of special importance for ceremonial magic, but it also enhances any work with omens and symbolism in general. As is well known, the ceremonial magician operates with a great variety of symbols, glyphs and images (pentagram, hexagram, elemental weapons, figures of archangels, etc.), even if s/he may generally prefer sigils like the ones here described. Moreover, symbol-logical thinking is of importance in *any* magician's work, regardless which system s/he uses.[22] By working with images instead of intellectual concepts (even if our glyphs might stand for these concepts), we activate our unconscious and the source of our personal Magis.

But the real value of the Alphabet of Desire lies in two different qualities of energy that exist while we are using it. Both can be explained only to a point in everyday language, which is why I must beg you to accept the following remarks as nothing more than a tentative approach towards something essentially ineffable.

To start with, we should keep in mind that repetition of certain techniques rarely fails to impress the unconscious, vide the effects of positive thinking, autosuggestion, autohypnosis, and Mantra usage. Our mantric sigils work on the same principle. With the Alphabet of Desire, we create an arsenal of *reusable* sigils which are implanted anew and additionally with each operation. Spare, for example, developed the sigil for the introduction of will ("I desire" =) which he then combined with other parts of his sentences of desire. This may suffice as an example of reusable sigils. Since we cannot deal with the whole of Spare's magical philosophy here, I don't want to go further into his numerous abstract sigils, which can only be understood in connection with his rather complex system (e.g., sigils for the "empirical Ego" or the "possessive Being"). However, it must be mentioned that there is far more to a symbolic language than a purely mechanical collation of nouns mounted in images. You will also need verbs like "doing," "healing," "destroying," etc., and conjunctions like "and," "therefore," "but," etc., will prove themselves very useful in practical work. As to these latter glyphs, Spare employed sigils (or, rather, more accurately, parts of sigils) such as ⟋⟋ ⟋ ⟋⟋⟋ (for plural forms), etc.

Let us assume that you want to perform a sigil operation with the following sentence of desire:

THIS MY WISH FOR B. TO OBTAIN
HEALTH AND STRENGTH.

Let us further assume that for the particles of the sentence "This my wish," "Health," "Strength" and "to obtain" you have already developed finished sigils such as the following:

THIS IS MY WISH=   HEALTH=

STRENGTH=   AND=

FOR=

All that remains now is an individual sigil for your patient B., which you might develop by employing the word method. Let us assume you have obtained the following glyph: ⊖⊖ .

Now we have the whole image or glyphical text:

You may put a frame around it:

This would be the finished sigil or, more accurately, the sigil sentence. Activation/internalizing follows the usual method. Theoretically, the several parts of the sigil may be merged and simplified even more, but this effort would hardly be justified. A simple sigil developed with the word or pictorial method would work quite as easily without all this bother. The demand for the preferably most simple end sigil finds its limitations here.

Last, but not least, the Alphabet of Desire may be applied like all the other types of sigils discussed here, a point which pleases many a magician (dependent on temperament). Its possibilities are not exhausted in the slightest by this. In general, it can be said that the Alphabet of Desire should not so much serve concrete success magic but enhance experience (and creation) of oneself, of the internal universe, and of its structure in images. Since the Alphabet of Desire will most likely consist of philosophical terms like "truth," "cognition," "karma," etc., with which the unconscious is less familiar because of their abstract quality, a repeated or multiple usage of the sigils of the alphabet will, as experience has shown, assure success more surely than when used with the more uncomplicated sigils discussed before.

Spare himself has made a point in his *Book of Pleasure* (p. 50, comment 3) that different methods of constructing sigils will activate different levels of the psyche. Unfortunately, he failed to enlarge on this any further. In practice, you will see that this is certainly the case, in that different methods of constructing and charging sigils have a dissimilar feel to them, which means that they have different energy qualities. In my opinion, it is as yet too early to develop hierarchical structure and graded models for the theory of sigils at this stage of exploration as long as there is not enough empirical material available covering, as it should, the experiences of a large variety of sigil magicians. Most likely, as with the structuring principles explained in this chapter, a far more personal, individual schema will be called for in this area. But only time will tell.

Let us now take a look at the association technique for constructing the Alphabet of Desire and its function as a mirror of the psyche.

The Alphabet of Desire as a Mirror of the Psyche

The technique of *association* is basically a mixture of *automatic writing, the pictorial method*, and *meditation/intuition*. From the very beginning we can do without a scheme of order like the one we have seen in the last section. Instead, we will proceed according to situation, meaning that we will develop our sigil alphabet as we go along, combining the process with a bare minimum of conscious construction. Of course, we will employ some rationale in places, but generally we will proceed "chaotically" (one could even say "organically") rather than utilizing ratiocination, let alone deliberation. Let us look at two examples.

1st Example

You want to succeed on an academic examination by magical means. Your sentence of desire could be formulated like this: "THIS MY WISH TO PASS MY EXAMINATION WELL." Because you are fond of experimenting, you decide to use the Alphabet of Desire and develop it with the association technique. You get into a state of *active meditation* where you "implant" your questions. Which questions? There will be several because you will need a series of different sigils: one for the segment "THIS MY WISH," another one for "EXAMINATION," one for "TO PASS," and one for "WELL." (In a symbolic language like this, you may usually abandon "MY" with impunity. Keep in mind that the language should always be kept as simple as possible anyway, so as to enhance its symbolism and be nearer to its symbol-logic rationale.)

Now concentrate on the question of which sigil you should use in the future for the words "THIS MY WISH." Keep your pen on the paper and close your eyes. (If you prefer, you may write the words in capital letters at the top of the paper.) Empty your mind, thus creating a state of non-thinking. (If you want to proceed precisely and carefully, you might as well construct a mantrical sigil for your question and take it into your state of heightened awareness, achieving the latter by prolonged chanting.) After a while, the pen in your hand will start moving, seemingly by itself. When the movement stops, return from your meditation trance and open your eyes. You may find nothing but a scribble since your unconscious has yet to get acquainted with this method of communication. Here again, the completion of the Alphabet of Desire requires a great deal of patience and effort. Repeat this procedure until you are satisfied with the result. You don't have to scribble on the paper for hours; a few minutes will do. You may also cut around parts of the "scribbling" and form a sigil as in Figure 24 :

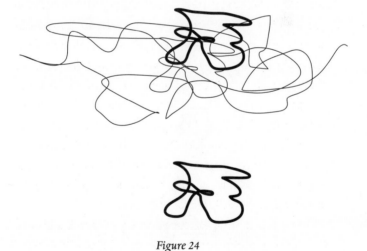

Figure 24

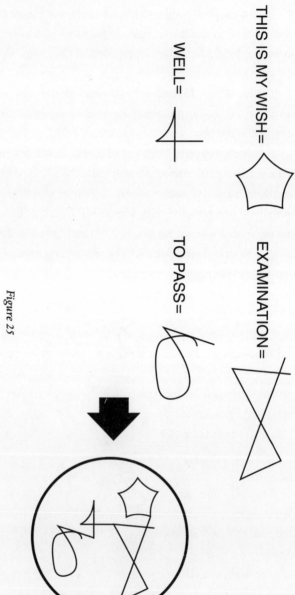

Figure 25

Admittedly, this sigil might not seem very simple, but you are free to experiment until you come across a more satisfying form. But do not, I repeat, do not try to control the process consciously!

Repeat this procedure with the other segments of the sentence. Let us assume that eventually you obtain the results of Figure 25.

You probably have noticed that these examples bear a certain resemblance to signatures and glyphs known from medieval books of spells. Perhaps, then as today, people were fond of employing the technique of automatic writing for their construction.

You should keep the sigils obtained by this method in a special "dictionary" for later use.

2nd Example

Suppose that some time later you wish to get a proper job (perhaps after your examination, which you have, of course, passed). However, you don't want to specify the precise type and location (company, department, etc.) of your job in order to retain a certain element of choice. Thus, you may formulate:

THIS MY WISH TO GET A PROPER JOB.

The words "A" and "TO GET" are not really needed. Your experience with the Alphabet of Desire is beginning to pay off, for now you will need only two additional sigils, one for "JOB" and another for "PROPER," the others having been constructed already in your previous working.

By the same method as before, you may obtain the following sigil for "JOB": 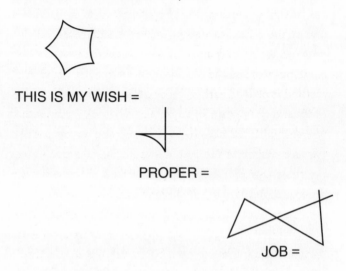 . (Since "well" and "proper" can mean the same thing, basically, you may again use the sigil from the last example. ─┼─ .)

THIS IS MY WISH =

PROPER =

JOB =

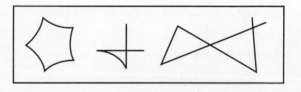

Figure 26

The material available for the construction of your sigil is shown in Figure 26.

In time, you will spend less and less effort on constructing (or "receiving") single sigils because your arsenal, or sigil dictionary, will grow larger and larger. This is one of the main advantages of this method, which also provides for regular and direct communication between consciousness and the unconscious. Unlike the structuring method explained earlier, you can do without schemes of order and can obtain sigils on an ad hoc basis, providing yourself with the possibility of using the list of your sigils as a mirror of the psyche even more effectively than the most carefully kept Magical Diary. Once you have marked several dozen or hundreds of sigils along with their respective meanings in your "dictionary," you have also acquired a complete overview of your magical work to date. This might sound a bit trivial, but if you take a look at your list after three or four years of practice, working through it systematically, you will be surprised how much inside information it actually contains. This will beat many a meditation session!

You should also meditate frequently upon the following: do most of your sigils really correspond to what you want from life and magic? (Have a look at the frequency with which you use them by keeping a tally.) Do you notice any imbalances? Which terms/aims appear least frequently? What should, according to your personal philosophy, be emphasized, at least theoretically? What is missing? Which emotions have you avoided and why? Thus, you can kill two birds with one stone by combining pragmatic-empirical practice with individual ethics.

The Alphabet of Desire is at its best when it comes to usefulness and variety of applications, and not only, as already mentioned, in the areas of self-recognition, growing knowledge, and self-analysis, but also in working with what Spare tagged "Atavistic nostalgia." The next chapter will be dedicated to this most fascinating aspect of sigil magic.

Chapter 7

Working with Atavistic Nostalgia

The term *Atavistic nostalgia* is another name for a principle which plays an important part in Spare's system and which is sometimes also defined as *Atavistic resurgence*. We can take but a quick glance at it here, for otherwise we would be obliged to give a complete introduction into Spare's entire system, which is not the purpose of this volume. Thus, we shall concentrate on the basic structures of Atavistic nostalgia and its possible applications in practical sigil magic.

The fundamental rationale of this practice is Darwin's Theory of Evolution. I'm sure you are familiar with Darwin's theory that man is but the momentary end-product of a long process of evolution that has been going on for millions of years and which has led from unicellular organisms and reptiles to mammals, including ourselves. Unlike popular "Vulgar Darwinism" (which was mainly monitored by the Church), Darwin did not so much claim that "man derives from monkey" but rather that we carry in us the entire heritage of *all* life forms and that we literally *incorporate* it. This "carrying in us" has been proved, for the most part, by modern genetics as well as by anthropology, physiology, and other disciplines of human biology, although Darwin's theories underwent tremendous transformations and challenges within the last 150 years.

For example, the human brain did not develop steadily and smoothly. Instead, it shows several added variations in the form of "accretions" in the course of evolution so that in fact we unite "various" brains in our skull. These derive in part from very early stages of evolution, e.g., the so-called "interbrain" (diencephalon), or "reptilian brain", or brainstem. Once again, it would lead us away from the matter at hand to discuss the pros and cons of Darwin's theory or repeat all the objections which have been raised against Darwinism (e.g., by the partisans of the rival theory of Lamarck). In our context, it is merely important to note that, in Spare's paradigm, *our entire evolutionary history is still organically present in us.* In other words, it is not as if we are completely finished with our former evolutionary stages, as if we had totally overcome them and laid them aside. Quite the contrary, in fact. The information of these earlier stages of our development is stored in our genes up to the present day and, according to Spare and many other magicians, it may be revitalized and tapped. (The parallels to Carl G. Jung's concept of the collective unconscious—at least in one of its possible interpretations—should be obvious.) This is exactly what happens with atavism, which in biology denotes a retrogression of sorts into earlier stages of evolution.

The term *nostalgia* calls for some clarification. Spare uses the English word *nostalgia* (New Latin *nostalgia),* deriving from the Greek *notos* = "homecoming" and *algos* = "pain"; thus, "homesickness" is one of its meanings. It is also related to Old English *genesan* = "survive" and to old German *ginesan* of the same meaning; Gothic *ganisan* = "being saved (healed)" also reveals Spare's frame of reference when using this term. He does not use the word so much in the sense of "longing for something (the source)," although this may be included as well, but rather he employs it to signify an act of conscious revitalization of old, archaic structures of the consciousness.

Consequently, Spare tried to go back into early, pre-human stages of consciousness by activating *genetic* or *hereditary memory.* This, for him, was not an end in itself, for his basic premise was that our greatest magical power, probably even the source of magic itself, lies hidden in these early stages of evolution. This assumption is continued if we take a look at the practices of Siberian or South American shaman or various African fetish priests, e.g., work with power animals, animal clan totems, etc. Practice also confirms this over and over again. Only when the magical will (which Spare is fond of calling "belief") has become "organic," meaning *unconscious and carnal,* is it, according to Spare, most effective. The deeper we go into our magical trance, returning to earlier stages of consciousness, the easier it will be for us to partake of its magical power and, most importantly, to direct and use it.

Nevertheless, it must be mentioned here that such a procedure demands a *great* deal of magical experience and a strong psychic stability. And let us not forget that with Atavistic nostalgia we enter pre-human stages of life, which, when brought to consciousness, may have catastrophic results. Thus, you might realize that not only your whole world-view but all your usual ideas about morals and ethics might be drastically changed by Atavistic nostalgia. You might be completely overwhelmed by your animal-consciousness (for example, your "reptilian karma," etc.) or even become obsessed, which could result in particularly unpleasant consequences in our bourgeois, conventional society. On the other hand, this entirely meets Sigmund Freud's demand "Where Id was, Self shall become" and belongs, in Carl G. Jung's terminology, to the challenge of the "shadow" and thus to individuation itself. But you should always realize that you are dealing with extremely hazardous powers, and if you have the slightest doubt whether you are ready for this, by all means, keep away from it, unless you are keen to experience one hellish trip after another.

Spare did not leave us any accurate directives on how to deal with Atavistic nostalgia, but his magical pictures and steles (to which he usually added handwritten explanations and reflections) give us some idea about his possible mode of approach. As is to be expected, he achieved these changes in consciousness by employing sigils.

There are several methods of Atavistic nostalgia. For example, we may shift our consciousness into that of dif-

ferent animals by constructing and activating proper sigils. Spare is fond of the term *karma* in this respect, but his
karma differs somewhat from the usual meaning of the
word. Karma in his terminology means the "sum of all experiences." Thus, we may, for example, create sigils from
the following sentences of desire:

—I WANT TO EXPERIENCE THE KARMA OF A CAT.

—THIS MY WISH TO OBTAIN THE CONSCIOUS-
NESS OF A BIRD OF PREY.

—THIS MY DESIRE TO BECOME A UNICELLULAR
ORGANISM IN MY DREAMS.

In regard to the first sentence of desire, Pete Carroll
in *Liber Null & Psychonaut* mentions incredible results (p.
203.) It is advisable, especially in the beginning, to experience atavisms in states of dream *only*, until you have
become more familiar with them. Only then should you
experience atavisms in everyday life and, of course, in
rituals. You could append the word "immediately" to the
above sentences and then charge pentacles or steles with
the help of the Alphabet of Desire for use in ritual for special workings (e.g., as "gateways" to an altered state of
awareness). Again, this method calls for a lot of training
and experience.

Another method consists of phrasing the sentence of
desire less specifically but more comprehensively. This
method should be understood as an *augmentation* to the
aforementioned procedure and not as an alternative. Here
again are some examples for sentences of desire:

—THIS MY WISH TO EXPERIENCE MY ATAVISMS.

—THIS MY WISH TO EXPERIENCE
THE STAGES BEFORE MY BIRTH.

—THIS MY WISH TO EXPERIENCE
THE SOURCE OF MY LIFE.

—THIS MY WISH TO EXPERIENCE MY REPTILE
INCARNATIONS IN RITUAL.

The key words "reptile incarnations" show that we are moving close to another technique of regression—reincarnation therapy. But the intention of the sigil magician is different insofar as s/he employs atavisms to charge sigils further or to start magical operations. For example, a talisman charged while one is in a "reptile consciousness" will work more powerfully than a talisman charged while in a state of normal magical trance. Of course, we must bear in mind that all of these atavistic states of consciousness have their own shortcomings and strong points. It would be downright foolish to demand highly intellectual work from a reptile with its small, barely developed brain. The incarnation of a bird won't be suitable to give us a lot of knowledge about life underwater, and the karma of a fish is not responsible for problems of hunting in the steppes or buying a car (though it may be excellent for buying a submarine!). We have to learn to choose and to employ these specialists in the optimal manner.

Working with animals has a long magical tradition and most "primitive" peoples still do this. Even a "city magi-

cian" like Franz Bardon recommends it on the fourth level
of the "magical mental training" in his book *Initiation into
Hermetics*. Sujja Su'a'No-ta also covers it in the first part of
her book *Element-Magie*. Remember the witches' familiars
to which such inordinate attention was given in the time
of the Inquisition. Modern technology has largely succeeded in subduing the animal aspects in our lives. Thus,
this magical art has nearly disappeared in our culture. On
the other hand, we can, with its help, create a good coun-
terbalance to the modern tendency of overemphasizing
artificiality and technology.

It will usually take years of practice until you are ready
to work with atavistic nostalgia in a predictable and reli-
able way. As a species, we had to struggle much too hard
for evolution, so our consciousness and our censor will
not stand by unflinchingly and watch as we scratch off
our civilizing varnish, risking the possibility of destroying
everything again. One reason why true mastership in this
practice can only be achieved after many years lies in the
fact that during this period, a stabilization of the whole
psyche has to be achieved. If not, our brain could never
handle experiences which are dead, similar to Lovecraftian
tales. Furthermore, if we endorse the evolutionary model,
a new step in evolution must always be guaranteed or our
own genetic alarm mechanisms would destroy the whole
system of our organism. Finally, in evolutionary terms
we are little more than parts of a general organism which
cannot afford to allow uncontrolled regressions to a larger
extent. Therefore, we will have to "offer" something to
this general organism (when seen as a personification) for

its collective development. Only then will we be able to use its huge power resources.

Despite all the dangers which are entangled with the use of specific or less specific animated atavisms, a small number of magicians will always consider this to be the crown of their art and one of their highest aspirations. Today is the product of yesterday, and if we are inclined to take the gnostic questions "Who am I?," "Where do I come from?," and "Where do I go to?" seriously, we cannot afford to do without the sheer unlimited knowledge to be gained from this practice. Atavism leads us back to the source of all life, regardless of whether we call it the Big Bang, God, Ain, Bythos, Chaos, or whatever we like. In this respect, the magic of the "re-animated atavisms" also represents a mystical and philosophical method, a method which chooses the path "directly through the flesh" instead of, as is regular Western practice, employing the spirit only, without appreciating the vessel which enables its existence in the first place. To complete the picture, it must be mentioned that sigil magic is not the only magical way. Thus, the "path of carnal memory" may easily be combined with purely mental and mystical paths, if this is preferred.

Atavistic nostalgia offers us a variety of aspects which have yet to be explored. Here we find virgin land which has been waiting for millions of years to be discovered and charted!

Finally, I would like to mention that present experience has shown that sigils created with the pictorial method as well as the Alphabet of Desire do better in atavistic nostalgia than other glyphs. The reason for this might be that these methods are somewhat more "pristine" (at least they appear to be so to us), but, of course, this may only correspond to subjective structures. Nevertheless, I urgently advise experimenting with the Alphabet of Desire in this field because here its abilities can be developed to the fullest and because its energy seems to be best adapted to this line of magic. Working with a structured alphabet provides us with the additional advantage that our experience may gain more stability and, in some cases, more substantiality. On the other hand, an associatively constructed alphabet often provides us with very powerful, instantly successful, sigils because its glyphs pop up even more "directly" from the unconscious and the hereditary memory than those of other techniques with the possible exception of the pictorial method.

It's also true that these two different methods of constructing the alphabet may be combined with one another. Thus, we might, for example, (as did Spare) construct 22 basic glyphs (being the generic or basic terms) and then add any number of merely functional glyphs using the method of automatic association. There are no limits whatsoever to one's own desire for experimentation. Remember, who dares, wins.

Chapter 8

But How Does It Work?

You may have noticed that in previous explanations I frequently referred to the "unconscious" into which sigils are "implanted," after which they start working like good fairies. The unconscious makes sure that sigils "will flesh" (to use Spare's own term). Regarding this "incarnation," we must never forget that the sigils themselves play nothing but a secondary part in the overall process of magic. Spare even goes so far as to state that each evolutionary step has been an unconscious, literally "corporeal" act of will. Thus, for example, animals only started to develop wings when their desire to fly had become "organic." This may seem a weird proposition, but basically it is nothing but a rephrasing of the old theory that all creation is based on an act of will of the Godhead or of

Chaos, or incarnated Will. The sigil is the "flesh" of the magician's will, so its successes are "incarnations" of the glyph itself.

If we really want to explain why sigils start to work, we would have to explain magic as a whole, but, unfortunately, a lot of it is at sixes and sevens. It's not as if there were no explanatory models; indeed, they seem to come cheaper by the dozen. But they are nothing but just that—models which do not really prove anything; in the best cases, they only illustrate the process. Back in the earliest days of psychology (which is still struggling for acknowledgment as a "science") there existed a model of explanation for the human soul which has its shortcomings but still serves us rather well. I am referring to the model of the *consciousness,* the *censor,* and the *unconscious.* Furthermore, there is the *Id,* the *Self,* and the *Superego.* Some writers differentiate even more accurately between the unconscious and the subconscious, etc., but the model *consciousness/unconsciousness/censor* has become established nearly everywhere. But this, as said before, is only a model and not a scientifically objectified fact in the sense of physics or any other "exact" science. Neither Freud nor Jung went so far—as many modern occultists tend to do— to confuse an explanatory model with a law of nature.

Certainly, Spare may be accused of having stuck too closely to what was in those days (1909–1913, when the *Book of Pleasure* was written) Freud's brand-new psychoanalytic model. If we read Spare's attempts at an explanation, we get the impression of a near fanatic hostility against the consciousness. In his opinion, only the unconscious possesses magical abilities and powers. This is the reason why he stresses so strongly the necessity of forgetting sigils. The consciousness is considered a continuously lurking enemy which has to be parried all the time.

This may have been justified in Spare's days, and maybe it still is. Many a sigil magician have come to the conclusion that it is best to construct a multitude of sigils, let them lie around for weeks or months, and activate/internalize them only when the contents (and the purpose for which they have been constructed) have been completely forgotten. This technique seems to be reasonable, but then, of course, it is suited only for long-term operations. Nevertheless, it cannot be denied that sigils are more effective in relation to how completely they have been obliterated from consciousness.

Ray Sherwin has presented an explanatory model which is quite enticing.[23]

To explain the illustration it should be mentioned that Sherwin considers the Holy Guardian Angel (cf. the Abramelin system) as being the psychic censor (a somewhat unconventional interpretation which has its source in Chaos Magic). The term *Kia* is taken from Spare's system and is explained by Sherwin's description of point *k*.

Now, *a* and *b* join to construct the sigil, which then has to be implanted in *d*. If *d* refuses to accept the sigil, it is probably because it does not understand it. The reason may be that it is either too complicated or that *a* and *b* use symbols, pictographs, and ideograms which are not compatible with those of *d*. Sherwin points out that, according to Aleister Crowley, only a magician who is capable of direct communication with the Holy Guardian Angel will achieve a direct connection to the unconscious. The

altered state of awareness, *c,* marks the point of intersection between *a*, *b*, and *d*. It may switch off the censor completely and thereby provide direct contact between these
areas of the psyche.

Sherwin's Model

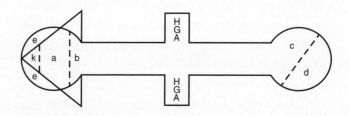

a = Ego, Will, Belief
b = Awareness, Perception
Consciousness: Individuality, Awakeness
HGA = The Holy Guardian Angel =
    Censorship Mechanism

Reactive Mechanisms

c = Altered Consciousness,
    "liminal state of consciousness"
d = Sub/Unconsciousness, Sleep, True Will
e = Macrocosm, Chaos
k = Kia, Soul, Individuality without Ego

To begin with, this model suffers, like most models do,
from being overly one-sided. It pretends that the barrier
of the censor is absolute, a "semi-permeable" membrane
or filter which permits movement in one direction only
(from *d* to *a/b*) while blocking everything in the opposite
direction. This is certainly an exaggeration because within

this model we could not explain why conscious percep-
tions may be stored in the unconscious (a fact which our
dreams prove all the time with their digestion of the day's
unresolved events; the same can be said for our memory
and our programmed emotions, etc.). Furthermore, it
does not take into account that the unconscious is en-
gaged all the time and in all human acts, even when consciously constructing a sigil. After all, it is the only part of
our psyche which is active 24 hours a day (as opposed to
consciousness which needs its daily breaks), encompassing
the stage of the consciousness.

Next, I would like to introduce two more models of
my own, which also have shortcomings, but might help to
illustrate the whole procedure.

Even though the threshold of the censor in Model A is
seen as (if only slightly) more permeable than in Sherwin's
model, there is usually no (or just a minor) direct contact
between consciousness and unconsciousness. (Imagine it
to be like a sieve, where only the smallest particles can slip
through the holes.) The channel of ecstasy goes around
the filter of the censor, and the pressure of ecstasy (meaning magical trance) gets rid of the membranes at the
mouths of consciousness as well as of unconsciousness for
a limited period of time. Thus, it creates the possibility for
an exchange "on a large scale" whereby the shield of reality,
i.e., the limited area of perception and evaluation which are
required for normal everyday reality, is bypassed and sometimes even undermined. This model is purely intra-psychic
and does not explain why altered states of consciousness
or whatever type of communication between consciousness and unconsciousness (read MAGIC) may have an effect on the material plane.

Model A

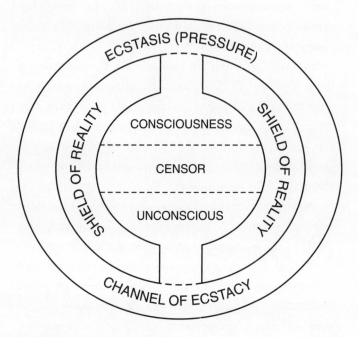

Such models are also termed psychologistic. I have followed them in this study for convenience and accessibility,
not because of any particular belief that magic can only
be explained in psychological terms.

Finally, I present another model (model B, page 104)
which has been adapted from Theosophy (and is still
widely appreciated in magic) and is oriented to the sphere
structure while also integrating the psychological pattern.

Levels, which have formerly been seen as hierarchically
stratified, are now understood as "states of oscillation"
overlying one another which, of course, cannot be illustrated in a two-dimensional drawing. The probes *a* are inlet
ventiles which work in both directions. Point *a'* is a double

probe through which not only the direct, censor-indepen-dent contact between consciousness and unconsciousness is controlled, but through which the consciousness also gets in direct contact with the mental sphere (while avoiding the censor-filter and the astral plane). Channel c is only permissible in a state of "altered awareness." The two "dream levels" of the consciousness and the unconsciousness have direct access to the astral level. (Lucid dreaming would imply an intersection point with the mental level, which is very rare.) To be effective, sigilization should take place in c (the altered state of consciousness). Be aware that the consciousness does not have direct access to the causal plane and the unconsciousness has only got indirect access to the physical level via the causal plane. According to the Theosophical model, the causal plane presides over all the other levels and controls them. On the causal level, the causes are planted by magical means, which often manifest themselves on the physical level as "unexplained miracles," "strange coincidences," etc.—everything we understand as magic.

Eventually, such models do not have any real value of cognition; all we are doing is trying to explain the unknown (in this case, the way in which magic works) by the suspected (here, the structure of the psyche), achieving, however, little more but illustrations. Nevertheless, such illustrations are quite useful to satisfy our reason and to soften the censor, which in one way or another truly seems to exist. (One could also term it the "unknown barrier" that makes it difficult for us to seize and manipulate the magical universe.) Of course, we may quite consciously rape our own reason to achieve a gnostic trance. This, for example, is practiced by the order of the Jesuits

Model B

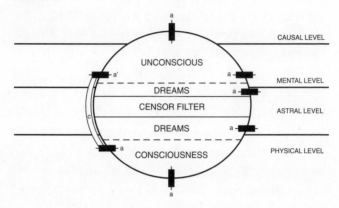

a = "ventile" or "probe"
a' = "double ventile" or "probe"
c = channel of communication / altered state of awareness

with its magical technique of the *"credo quia absurdum est"* ("I believe in it *because* it is absurd"), as does Rinzai Zen with its koans, but in doing so we are already returning to the field of procedural techniques, leaving the area of rational cognition.

If you find it fun to do so, you might develop your own models of explaining magic. This would have the advantage of establishing a stronger commitment to magic in your consciousness and unconscious (to remain persistently within psychologism), thus making it easier for magic to be integrated in everyday life. But don't forget that this is nothing but an—admittedly quite amusing—way of fiddling around.

You may perhaps be a bit disappointed now if you had expected to find the final explanation for magic, life, the universe, and everything in this chapter. In that case, try to get over it with one of Crowley's favorite aphorisms: "He who knows the HOW does not care about the WHY." You can achieve certainty over the HOW mainly through practice—and practice is much more productive anyway than vague speculations of dubious value.

Chapter 9

Constructing Sigils
with Planetary Cameas

M agical squares, or cameas, are often used as a basis
for the construction of individual sigils. In fact,
the traditional sigils for planetary spirits and demons have
been cabbalistically constructed with the help of these
cameas. Since this technique belongs to yet another important branch of sigil magic and is relatively unknown, it
shall be covered here.

The following explanations are based on Israel Regardie's excellent book *How to Make and Use Talismans,*
which contains a very clear summary, though the author
refers to the older material of the Golden Dawn and other
writers have explained the system elsewhere.[24] To be able

to use these systems, however, you need a sound basic knowledge of cabbalism and planetary magic. Unfortunately, these cannot be taught here and would lead away from our main topic. Readers who are quite unfamiliar with these disciplines should refer to the relevant literature listed in the bibliography.

The basis of this method of constructing sigils is the *Aiq Bekr,* also labeled the "Kabbalah of the Nine Chambers." Each letter of the Hebrew alphabet is equivalent to a numerical value. The alphabet with its assigned numerical values is seen on the next page.

These letters are arranged in nine "chambers" according to their decimal values:

Shin	Lamed	Gimel	Resh	Kaph	Beth	Qoph	Yod	Aleph
ש	ל	ג	ר	כ	ב	ק	י	א
300	30	3	200	20	2	100	10	1
Final Mem	Samekh	Vau	Final Kaph	Nun	Heh	Tau	Mem	Daleth
ם	ס	ו	ך	נ	ה	ת	מ	ד
600	60	6	500	50	5	400	40	4
Final Tzaddi	Tzaddi	Teth	Final Peh	Peh	Cheth	Final Nun	Ayin	Zain
ץ	צ	ט	ף	פ	ח	ן	ע	ז
900	90	9	800	80	8	700	70	7

א	A	1		Aleph
ב	B, V	2		Beth
ג	G, Gh	3		Gimel
ד	D, Dh	4		Daleth
ה	H	5		He
ו	O, U, V	6		Vau
ז	Z	7		Zayin
ח	Ch	8		Cheth
ט	T	9		Teth
י	I, Y	10		Yod
כ	K, Kh	20, 500	ך	Kaph
ל	L	30		Lamed
מ	M	40, 600	ם	Mem
נ	N	50, 700	ן	Nun
ס	S	60		Samekh
ע	Aa, Ngh	70		Ayin
פ	P, Ph	80, 800	ף	Pe
צ	Tz	90, 900	ץ	Tzaddi
ק	Q	100		Qoph
ר	R	200		Resh
ש	S, Sh	300		Shin
ת	T, Th	400		Tau

Depending on the appropriate magical camea, sometimes it is necessary to reduce a numerical value so that the pertinent number in the camea can be touched when drawing the sigil. For example, look at the demon Bartzabel of the Mars sphere, following Regardie (p. 15). In Hebrew, this name is written (from right to left):

Lamed	Aleph	Beth	Tzaddi	Resh	Beth
30	1	2	90	200	2

The magical camea of Mars follows, one version in numbers, the other in Hebrew letters:

11	24	7	20	3
4	12	25	8	16
17	5	13	21	9
10	18	1	14	22
23	6	19	2	15

יא	כד	ז	כ	ג
ד	יב	כה	ח	יו
יז	ה	יג	כא	ט
י	יח	א	יד	כב
כג	ו	יט	ב	יה

You will note that the numbers 200, 90, and 30 do not appear in the magical square; deleting the zeros in our demon's name gives us 2, 9, and 3. Thus, we get the following order of numbers (again from right to left): 3/1/2/9/2/2.

Usually the sigil begins with a curlicue and ends with a stroke. If any one number is covered twice, two arcs are drawn. Let's have a look at this sigil in its camea in Figure 27.

In this example, the traditional sigils really have been constructed consciously.

To complete the picture, the following pages consist of the magical cameas of the planets together with the sigils of their intelligences and demons, as well as the planetary seals, which have been developed with a very similar but slightly different method.

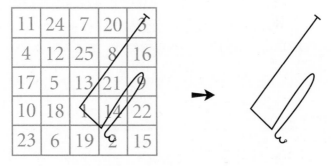

Figure 27

Beside each numbered camea you will find a square containing the Hebrew letters according to their numerical values, which may save you a lot of trouble constructing your sigils in the Hermetic tradition. The illustrations are taken from Agrippa's classic work *De Occulta Philosophia* (Vol. 2, 1533).

The rule of marking the beginning and the end of a planetary sigil, namely to start with a curlicue and to end with a stroke, has not been followed throughout. This may be due to Agrippa's intention of preventing any possible abuse. By marking the beginning and the end of such a sigil we have all the directional information necessary to draw it in evocation (with the exception of the composed sigils). I have deliberately not "corrected" the sigils because I wanted to present the traditional form without any changes of my own. Furthermore, these corrections might confuse those readers unfamiliar with the subject if they suddenly come across different versions of one and the same sigil in other traditional books. For practice, however, I advise you to redraw the sigils and correct them where necessary.

THE MAGICAL CAMEAS OF THE PLANETS ("TABLES") AND THE SEALS AND SIGILS OF THE PLANETARY POWERS, INTELLIGENCES, AND DEMONS.

(following Agrippa of Nettesheim, *De Occulta Philosophia*, Vol. 2, 1533)

Table of Saturn

Numbers			Hebrew Letters		
4	9	2	ד	ט	ב
3	5	7	ג	ה	ז
8	1	6	ח	א	ו

Seals or Characters

of Saturn   his Intelligence   his Demon

Divine Names in accord with the numbers of Saturn

Numbers	Divine Names	in Hebrew
3	Ab	אב
9	Hod	הד
15	Yah	יה
15	Hod	הוד
45	Tetragrammaton Extended	יוד הא ואו הא
45	Agiel, Intelligence of Saturn	אגיאל
45	Zazel, Demon of Saturn	זאזל

Table of Jupiter

Numbers				Hebrew Letters			
4	14	15	1	ד	יד	טו	א
9	7	6	12	ט	ז	ו	יב
5	11	10	8	ה	יא	י	ח
16	2	3	13	יו	ב	ג	יג

Seals or Characters

of Jupiter   his Intelligence   his Demon

Divine Names in accord with the numbers of Jupiter

Numbers	Divine Names	in Hebrew
4	Abba	אבא
16		הוה
16		אהי
34	El Ab	אל אב
136	Iophiel, Intelligence of Jupiter	יהפיאל
136	Hismael, Demon of Jupiter	הסמאל

Table of Mars

Numbers   Hebrew Letters

11	24	7	20	3
4	12	25	8	16
17	5	13	21	9
10	18	1	14	22
23	6	19	2	15

יא	כד	ז	כ	ג
ד	יב	כה	ח	יו
יז	ה	יג	כא	ט
י	יח	א	יד	כב
כג	ו	יט	ב	יה

Seals or Characters

of Mars   his Intelligence   his Demon

Divine Names in accord with the numbers of Mars

Numbers	Divine Names	in Hebrew
5	**Heh, Letter of the Holy Name**	ה
25		יהי
65	**Adonai**	אדני
325	**Graphiel, Intelligence of Mars**	גראפיאל
325	**Bartzabel, Demon of Mars**	ברצאבאל

Table of the Sun

Numbers

6	32	3	34	35	1
7	11	27	28	8	30
19	14	16	15	23	24
18	20	22	21	17	13
25	29	10	9	26	12
36	5	33	4	2	31

Hebrew Letters

ו	לב	ג	לד	לה	א
ז	יא	כז	כח	ח	ל
יט	יד	יו	יה	כג	כד
יח	כ	כב	כא	יז	יג
כה	כט	י	ט	כו	יב
לו	ה	לג	ד	ב	לא

Seals or Characters

of the Sun   his Intelligence   his Demon

Divine Names in accord with the numbers of the Sun

Numbers	Divine Names	in Hebrew
6	**Vau, Letter of the Holy Name**	
6	**Prolonged Heh, Letter of the Holy Name**	הא
36	**Eloh**	אלה
111	**Nakhiel, Intelligence of the Sun**	נכיאל
666	**Sorath, Demon of the Sun**	סורת

Table of Venus

Numbers

22	47	16	41	10	35	4
5	23	48	17	42	11	29
30	6	24	49	18	36	12
13	31	7	25	43	19	37
38	14	32	1	26	44	20
21	39	8	33	2	27	45
46	15	40	9	34	3	28

Hebrew Letters

כב	מז	יו	מא	י	לה	ד
ה	כג	מח	יז	מב	יא	כט
ל	ו	כד	מט	יח	לו	יב
יג	לא	ז	כה	מג	יט	לז
לח	יד	לב	א	כו	מד	כ
כא	לט	ח	לג	ב	כז	מה
מו	יה	מ	ט	לד	ג	כח

Seals or Characters
  of Venus   her Intelligences   her Demon

Divine Names in accord with the numbers of Venus

Numbers	Divine Names	in Hebrew
7	**Aha**	אהא
49	**Hagiel, Intelligence of Venus**	הגיאל
175	**Kedemel, Demon of Venus**	קדמאל
1225	**Beni Seraphim, Intelligences of Venus**	בני שרפים

Table of Mercury

Numbers

8	58	59	5	4	62	63	1
49	15	14	52	53	11	10	56
41	23	22	44	45	19	18	48
32	34	35	29	28	38	39	25
40	26	27	37	36	30	31	33
17	47	46	20	21	43	42	24
9	55	54	12	13	51	50	16
64	2	3	61	60	6	7	57

Hebrew Letters

ח	נח	נט	ה	ד	סב	סג	א
מט	יה	יד	נב	נג	יא	י	נו
מא	כג	כב	מד	מה	יט	יח	מח
לב	לד	לה	כט	כח	לח	לט	כה
מ	כו	כז	לז	לו	ל	לא	לג
יז	מז	מו	כ	כא	מג	מב	כד
ט	נה	נד	יב	יג	נא	נ	יו
סד	ב	ג	סא	ס	ו	ז	נז

Seals or Characters
    of Mercury   his Intelligence   his Demon

Divine Names in accord with the numbers of Mercury

Numbers	Divine Names	in Hebrew
8	**Asboga, prolonged number eight**	אזבוגה
64	**Din**	דין
64	**Dani**	דני
260	**Tiriel, Intelligence of Mercury**	טיריאל
2080	**Taphthartharath, Demon of Mercury**	תפתרתרת

Table of the Moon

Numbers

37	78	29	70	21	62	13	54	5
6	38	79	30	71	22	63	14	46
47	7	39	80	31	72	23	55	15
16	48	8	40	81	32	64	24	56
57	17	49	9	41	73	33	65	25
26	58	18	50	1	42	74	34	66
67	27	59	10	51	2	43	75	35
36	68	19	60	11	52	3	44	76
77	28	69	20	61	12	53	4	45

Hebrew Letters

לז	עח	כט	ע	כא	סב	יג	נד	ה
ו	לח	עט	ל	עא	כב	סג	יד	מו
מז	ז	לט	פ	לא	עב	כג	נה	יה
יו	מח	ח	מ	פא	לב	סד	כד	נו
נז	יז	מט	ט	מא	עג	לג	סה	כה
כו	נח	יח	נ	א	מב	עד	לד	סו
סז	כז	נט	י	נא	ב	מג	עה	לה
לו	סח	יט	ס	יא	נב	ג	מד	עו
עז	כח	סט	כ	סא	יב	נג	ד	מה

Seals or Characters
of the Moon   her Demon

her Supreme Demon   her Supreme Intelligence

              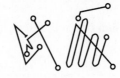

Divine Names in accord with the numbers of the Moon

Numbers	Divine Names	in Hebrew
9	Hod	הד
81	Elim	אלים
369	Chasmodai, Demon of the Moon	חשמודאי
3321	Shed Barshemath Sharthathan, Supreme Demon of the Moon	שדברשהמעת שרתתן
3321	Malka be-Tarshishim ad be-Ruah Shehaqim, Supreme Intelligence of the Moon	מלכא בתרשיתים עד ברוח שחקים

Individual sigils (for example, your first name) may be formed by using the same system. To do so, the name has to be transferred into Hebrew, which, of course, demands some previous experience. Once you have defined the numerical value of the name, the sigil is made by going over the chosen planetary camea. Obviously, the same name will have a completely different design in the seven different cameas.

Now if we, for example, assign the purpose of a special sigil operation to a specific planetary sphere, we can, with this method of construction, *assume the identity of the chosen sphere.* Let us take a magician whose magical name is MERLIN. In Hebrew, this would be written in the following manner (from right to left):

(Final-)

NUN	YOD	LAMED	RESH	MEM
700	10	30	200	40

He now wants to perform some aggressive operation, e.g., a magical attack. Thus, he will choose the camea of the Mars sphere as his basic matrix. This results (after the proper reduction of the numbers) in:

= **MARS IDENTITY**

He might also use this sigil in combination with the Alphabet of Desire for his operation, or he might integrate it into a word or pictorial sigil, etc.

If, however, he wanted to be successful in a lawsuit, he would choose the Jupiter sphere and get the following sigil on the camea of Jupiter:

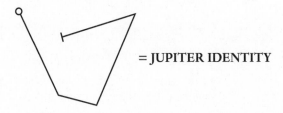

= JUPITER IDENTITY

It is always the same name, but *with* and *in* a different planetary vibration. By the same method, we may transfer reduced sentences of desire, words of power, etc., to the planetary system and sigilize them with the help of the cameas. If you already have some experience with planetary magic, you will immediately recognize the vast possibilities of this procedure.

Conclusion

I hope that I have provided you with ample practical hints in this brief introduction so that you can explore on your own the vast, fascinating area of sigil magic. Don't start off in a dogmatic spirit, though. Dare to experiment, make changes where you feel they may be necessary, and always aspire to develop your own techniques and methods. Sigil magic lives by the individuality of the magician; generally, people who stick to every letter of laws or rules make very little progress. Even though one of its major strong points lies in the field of success magic, sigil magic serves the individual's spiritual development as well. It can open completely new universes to us—an unlimited number of universes of experience—and eventually it will lead us back to the sources of magical power itself.

SALVE ATQUE VALE!

UBIQUE DAEMON ∴ UBIQUE DEUS ∴

Glossary

A∴A∴ —*Astrum Argentum* or Silver Star. A magical group founded by Aleister Crowley based on the teachings of the Hermetic Order of the Golden Dawn.

Abramelin system—A potent cabbalistic system of magic. It involves six months in prayer, following which you achieve "the Knowledge and Conversation of Your Holy Guardian Angel." This angel provides information on how to control demons so that they will bring you whatever you desire.

Agrippa—Henry Cornelius Agrippa von Nettesheim (1486–1535) was a famous alchemist, astrologer and magician. His *Three Books of Occult Philosophy or Magic* is considered to be a foundational work of the Western magical tradition.

Aiwass-revelation—In 1904, Aleister Crowley "received" *The Book of the Law,* a revelation from an entity referring to itself as Aiwass. The three short chapters in the book describe the end of the current aeon and the beginning and methods of the New Aeon.

Aleister Crowley—Born Edward Alexander Crowley (1875-1947), he is one of the most important and controversial magical writers and practitioners. He became a member of the Hermetic Order of the Golden Dawn but later left the order to found his own group, the A∴A∴. Later he joined the O.T.O. and became its head. A prolific writer, his magical system combined Western Cabbalistic magic with Eastern Tantra, Taoism, Buddhism and Yoga.

Chaos magic—Of recent origin, this system of magic focuses on personal symbolism rather than a traditional system. Experimental and free form, chaos is the field of potential from which we can tap magical forces.

Dogmatic magic—This type of magic forces a practitioner to use symbols and systems that may or may not be part of the magician's reality.

Fraternitas Saturni—The Brotherhood of Saturn is a German magical order. Highly secretive, some of their teachings are just coming to light.

Hermetic Order of the Golden Dawn—This group began operation in 1888 and fell victim to schism and strife in 1900. Its importance is in its unique combining of numerous magical systems into a coherent whole. Its membership included William Butler Yeats, Arthur Machen, Sax Rohmer, S.L. MacGregor Mathers, Dion Fortune, Aleister Crowley, Israel Regardie, A.E. Waite and numerous others.

IOT (The Magical Pact of the Illuminates of Thanateros)—The Pact is a loose conglomeration of groups and individuals practicing Chaos magic.

Koans—A Buddhist method for meditation, it involves giving the meditator an idea with no simple answer on which to contemplate. The most famous is "What is the sound of one hand clapping?"

Lao-Tse—Founder of Taoism.

Master Therion—A name used by Aleister Crowley under which he wrote several of his most important books, including *Magic in Theory and Practice*.

Mathers—Samuel Liddell MacGregor Mathers (1854–1918) was one of the founders of the Hermetic Order of the Golden Dawn and eventually became its sole leader. Through him came many of the unique and impressive rituals and magical techniques. The books he translated and edited on magic, including *The Sacred Magic of Abramelin the Mage, The Greater Key of Solomon* and *The Kabbalah Unveiled,* have helped many to become magicians. His autocratic nature lead to schisms in The Golden Dawn, and he eventually had magical wars with Aleister Crowley. He died in the influenza epidemic that rocked the world after World War I.

Nominalism—The philosophical belief that abstractions, generalities or universals have no objective reality, existing only as names.

O.T.O. (Ordo Templi Orientis; Order of Eastern Templars)—Founded in the late 1800s, it claimed to be associated with the Knights Templar and combined some fringe masonic traditions along with sex magic. Aleister Crowley became a member and later head of the order. He revamped it to match his magical ideas known as the Thelemic current. Numerous groups calling themselves O.T.O. have sprung up in recent years.

Ten Sephiroth—In Cabbalism (and Neo-Platonism), the universe is seen as being created through a series of emanations from the Godhead. In the Cabbalah these are known as the Ten Sephiroth and form a pattern called the Tree of Life. It is used by magicians for personal development, a key to astral travel, and a way to make correspondences for magic.

Thelemic concept—The system of magic propounded and advanced by Aleister Crowley.

Timothy Leary's and Robert Anton Wilson's circuits—Just as we have evolved, so has the "circuitry of our brains." We have eight circuits, and each can be opened by various means. Reaching a higher level allows a person greater personal and magical power, as well as greater awareness of the universe.

Wicca—An Old English word meaning "wise." Originally pronounced "Wee-Cha," it is the source for the more common word *witch*. Many Witches prefer the term Wicca as it does not have all of the negative connotations that many hundreds of years of defamation have placed on the word "witch."

Comments

1. One has only to think of the unfortunate development which occurred to a name like *Astarte* (Ishtar) in the course of centuries—an erstwhile Chaldean Moon Goddess developed in the Middle Ages via the addition of the plural ending "oth" into a male(!) demon with the name *Astaroth*. Today's evocatory magicians might be in for quite a surprise or two, if, for example, a supposedly male demon like Kedemel from the Venusian sphere suddenly appears before them as a female entity! (Quite obvious, actually, but who would have thought of it beforehand?)

2. Reprint from *Unicorn,* Issue 1/82, pp. 34–38.

3. Horst E. Miers does not mention him at all in his *Lexikon der Geheimwissenschaften* (Freiburg, 1970) [*Encyclopedia of the Occult Arts*], but this work is generally faulty in many other respects as well.

4. "Another English satanic occultist is Austin Osman Spare," *The Romantic Agony* (London, 2, 1970), p. 413, n.59.

5. The edition used here is a Canadian reprint by 93 Publishing (Montreal, 1975).

6. Kenneth Grant, *Images and Oracles of Austin Osman Spare* (York Beach, ME: Samuel Weiser, Inc., 1975).

7. First, numbers were assigned to the Hebrew letters, and second, the cameas, or magical number squares, were related to the different planets. For example, the names of the planetary intelligences were converted into numerical values and then the pertinent numbers in the squares were connected with one another, the whole resulting in a sigil. The late Israel Regardie gives a detailed introduction of this method in *How to Make and Use Talismans* (Wellingborough, Northamptonshire, England: The Aquarian Press, 1972 ff).

8. This term, which was coined by the author of this study, describes a certain type of magic which is based on subjective empiricism, or individual experiences without prior postulates. The opposite is Dogmatic magic, which demands a fair amount of faith from its practitioners, such as belief in the hierarchy of astral entities, correspondences, gnostic dualism, etc. We are not saying here that these concepts cannot be found at all in Pragmatic Magic but merely that they are only

considered as possible models of explanation amongst others of equal value. The Pragmatic magician is perfectly free to abandon them if s/he achieves the desired success without their help. S/he is, therefore, independent of so-called "revelations" of many a charlatan. On the other hand, of course, s/he cannot claim his/her experiences to be universal "truth." This prevents—at least ideally—the megalomania very common to practitioners of magic. A detailed discussion of these concepts remains to be covered by a larger, more specialized volume.

9. A facile way of looking at a subject like this quite often demands the use of illustration rather than differentiation. Thus, for example, the problem of reception cannot be dealt with here. It would certainly be an exaggeration to say that Spare influenced Pragmatic Magic directly. Rather, Pragmatists found him to be one of their ilk. Neither do we want to state that there are no Dogmatists left in the Anglo-Saxon countries. But the aforementioned writers, as is commonly known, are considered to be the leading thinkers of the magical scene of Great Britain, Canada, Australia and the USA.

10. The formula "THIS MY WILL TO ..." has proved to be very powerful in practice. Of course, it may be changed according to taste or even completely exchanged to any other formula. Practice has shown, however, that it is useful to begin every sigil working with the same formula because in the course of time the unconscious seems to respond to this with reflexive receptivity.

11. Ray Sherwin, writing as a former member of the IOT on a similar connection in his excellent *Theatre of Magic* (Leeds: The Sorcerer's Apprentice Press), introduces the term "Liminal Gnosis."

12. Compare the section "The Physiological Gnosis" and the subsequent explanations in *Liber Null* (York Beach, ME: Samuel Weiser, Inc., 1987), p. 33ff.

13. Kenneth Grant, *Images and Oracles of Austin Osman Spare* (York Beach, ME: Samuel Weiser, Inc., 1975).

14. Incidentally, this difficulty can even be used constructively should you encounter problems with visualizing or imagining objects or persons. For example, if you don't succeed in seeing a giraffe with closed eyes, try very intensely *not* to see one. Sometimes the spell is immediately broken by this simple trick.

15. Ray Sherwin, *The Book of Results* (Leeds: The Sorcerer's Apprentice Press), p. 34.

16. I should perhaps briefly point out that virgin parchment is not, as many people still seem wont to believe, tanned from the hymens of desperately destitute virgins! Instead, the skin of unborn calves is used for its manufacture. Since it is financially unprofitable to slaughter the mother cow or to induce an artificial abortion for obtaining it, only animals which have died in an accident, had to be put to sleep, or died a natural death can be exploited. This is why the most time-honored commodity of all Western magic is so rare. It is, therefore, very difficult to procure, especially since veterinary regulations in most countries pose an additional obstacle for its production. Its chief commercial

source of supply is the London parchment exchange. In extremely paper-thin form it is also utilized as "gold-beater's skin."

17. The letter *b* is missing in Peter Carroll's example—an obvious typesetting mistake which we have not corrected for the sake of correct quotation. This does not, however, invalidate the example as a whole.

18. Kenneth Grant, *Images and Oracles of Austin Osman Spare,* p. 59ff.

19. Marcus M. Jungkurth, *Zos Kia* (Berlin: Stein der Weisen, 1983), pp. 256–264.

20. Cf. Sujja Su'a'No-ta "Die Sprache des Unbewußten, Anleitung zur Erarbeitung einer individuellen Ritual-sprache" in *Unicorn,* III/82, pp. 137–141.

21. For example, refer to Sujja Su'a'No-ta's *ElementMagie* (Bad Honnef: Edition Magus, 1983), pp. 51–56.

22. Cf. my article "Mythen in Tüten. Vom magischen Umgang mit Analogien" in *Unicorn,* XI/84, pp. 221–229.

23. Ray Sherwin, *The Book of Results* (Leeds: The Sorcerer's Apprentice Press), p. 32ff.

24. See Timothy D'Arch Smith's introduction to Francis Barrett's *The Magus* (Secaucus, NJ: Citadel Press, 1977), pp. vi-vii. His explanation is a bit tricky. The magician places the figures of a magical camea in their numerical order (always from left to right, starting in the bottom row) in a camea. After this, he traces the numbers following their numerical order on the original camea. The result of the example given in his introduction, the Saturn glyph, is quite convincing. But in the case

of Jupiter and Mars, you need a good deal of imagination to recognize the proper glyph as given in the relevant classics in the resulting scribble. D'Arch Smith does point out, however, that some aesthetic corrections may have been made to obtain more or less symmetrical figures. Thus, his thesis is enlightening and witty and cannot be discarded completely, although a convincing presentation of the construction of *all* glyphs following this model might have provided more clarity to his procedures.

Bibliography

Aerosol. "Smuggling Sigils Across. Sigil Magic for the Professional Magician." *Chaos International,* 4 (1988) p. 10f.

Agrippa of Nettesheim. *De Occulta Philosophia.* Vol. 2, Köln, 1533.

Barrett, Francis, *The Magus or Celestial Intelligencer: A Complete System of Occult Philosophy.* Reprint with a new introduction by Timothy D'Arch Smith. Secaucus, NJ: Citadel Press, 1977.

Carroll, Peter. *Liber Null & Psychonaut.* York Beach, ME: Samuel Weiser, Inc., 1987.

Dukes, Ramsey. *Uncle Ramsey's Bumper Book of Magical Spells.* Unpub.

Frater U.·.D.·.. "Mythen in Tüten. Vom magischen Umgang mit Analogien." *Unicorn*, XI/84, pp. 221–229.

Grant, Kenneth. *Images and Oracles of Austin Osman Spare.* York Beach, ME: Samuel Weiser, Inc., 1975.

Jungkurth, Marcus M. *Zos Kia: Der Magier Austin Osman Spare und die Magie des Voodoo.* Berlin: Stein der Weisen, 1983.

Regardie, Israel. *How to Make and Use Talismans.* Wellingborough, Northamptonshire, England: The Aquarian Press, 1972.

Sherwin, Ray. *The Book of Results.* Leeds: The Sorcerer's Apprentice Press, n.d.

———. *The Theatre of Magic.* Leeds: The Sorcerer's Apprentice Press, n.d.

Spare, Austin Osman. *The Collected Works of Austin Osman Spare: His Art, Philosophy and Magic.* Ed. Christopher Bray and Peter Carroll. Leeds: The Sorcerer's Apprentice Press, 1982.

Su'a'No-ta, Sujja. *Element-Magie: Ein praktischer Leitfaden.* Introduction by Frater U.·.D.·.. Bad Honnef: Edition Magus, 1983.

———. "Die Sprache des Unbewußten. Anleitung zur Erarbeitung einer individuellen Ritualsprache." *Unicorn*, III/82, pp. 137–141.

To Write to the Author

If you wish to contact the author or would like more information about this book, please write to the author in care of Llewellyn Worldwide Ltd. and we will forward your request. Both the author and publisher appreciate hearing from you and learning of your enjoyment of this book and how it has helped you. Llewellyn Worldwide Ltd. cannot guarantee that every letter written to the author can be answered, but all will be forwarded. Please write to:

Frater U∴D∴
℅ Llewellyn Worldwide
2143 Wooddale Drive
Woodbury, MN 55125-2989

Please enclose a self-addressed stamped envelope for reply,
or $1.00 to cover costs. If outside the U.S.A., enclose
an international postal reply coupon.

Many of Llewellyn's authors have websites with additional information and resources. For more information, please visit our website at http://www.llewellyn.com.

High Magic

Theory & Practice

Frater U∴ D∴

Magic may be one of the most difficult, diversified, and fascinating of all the occult sciences. Understanding the theory behind this rich Western tradition is crucial to becoming an accomplished magician. This comprehensive and well-rounded introduction to magical practice provides a solid foundation for furthering one's magic studies.

Instead of issuing spells and rituals like a recipe book, this magic primer explains the basic laws governing magic. The author also discusses what it means to be a "good" magician, emphasizing self-discipline and training one's will, imagination, and trance abilities. Many facets of high magic are covered, including The Lesser Banishing Ritual of the Pentagram, sigil magic, ritual magic, visualization, the Greater Ritual of the Pentagram, planetary magic, tools of the magician, trance work, and much more.

978-0-7387-0471-5, 432 pp., 7½ x 9⅛,   **$31.95**

To order, call 1-877-NEW-WRLD
Prices subject to change without notice
Order at Llewellyn.com 24 hours a day, 7 days a week!

HIGH
MAGIC II

Theory   Practice
Expanded

Frater U∴D∴

High Magic II

Expanded Theory and Practice

FRATER U.'. D.'.

Europe's best-known ceremonial magician and contemporary occult author, Frater U.'. D.'. is back with the companion volume to his highly acclaimed *High Magic*. Previously unavailable in English, this advanced guide to high magic has been eagerly awaited by ceremonial magicians, mages, and hermetic practitioners.

High Magic II explores the theory and practice of a variety of types of magic, including mirror magic, mudras, sigil magic, shamanism, magical orders, folk magic, demonic magic, divination, and letter magic. The book also delves into magic and yoga, magic in the Bible, the practical Kabbalah, forms of initiation, and the magic of Ancient Egypt and the late Hellenistic period. Many provocative areas of magical practice are addressed, some of them for the first time in an English-language book.

978-0-7387-1063-1, 480 pp., 7½ x 9⅛   **$31.95**

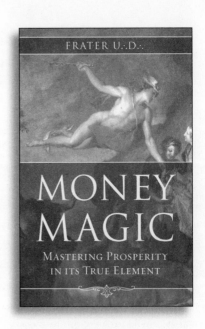

MONEY MAGIC

MASTERING PROSPERITY
IN ITS TRUE ELEMENT

FRATER U.∴D.∴

Money Magic

Mastering Prosperity in its True Element

FRATER U∴D∴

Europe's best-known ceremonial magician and contemporary occult author, Frater U∴D∴, presents the definitive guide to money magic. Previously unavailable in English, this advanced guide will be welcomed by ceremonial magicians, mages, and hermetic practitioners.

Money Magic starts with the revolutionary premise that money is an elemental energy. By transforming the idea of money in your psyche, you invite wealth to flow more freely and easily into your life. This comprehensive course gives step-by-step instructions on how to master prosperity in its true element using new paradigms, magical invocations, rituals, sigils, and pathworkings.

978-0-7387-2127-9, 240 pp., 5³⁄₁₆ x 8   **$16.95**

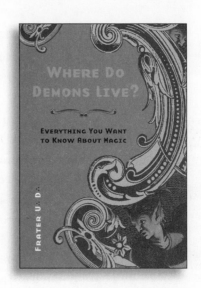

WHERE DO DEMONS LIVE?

EVERYTHING YOU WANT
TO KNOW ABOUT MAGIC

FRATER U∴D∴

Where Do Demons Live?

Everything You Want to Know About Magic

FRATER U∴D∴

Where do demons live? What's the skinny on sigils? Frater U∴D∴ plays Dear Abby for the occult crowd in this entertaining and informative romp through some of magic's commonly asked questions. The renowned European author and esoteric expert introduces us to chatty Aunt Klara, a straight-talking sorceress who answers burning questions on magical topics.

These bite-sized essays explore topics such as joining a magical order, the pros and cons of working with a magical master, poltergeists, and even the magical validity of the Harry Potter novels. Easy to page through, good-humored, and never dogmatic, *Where Do Demons Live?* is the perfect quick reference for beginning practitioners.

978-0-7387-1479-0, 216 pp., 5 x 7   **$15.95**

Crone's Book of Charms & Spells

VALERIE WORTH

Here is a charming little grimoire of magical practices and rituals that reads as if it were written in an earlier century. In a style that is poetic and appealing to the imagination, this book will give you practical directions for carrying out numerous spells, charms, recipes, or rituals—all of which take their inspiration from nature and folklore.

Concoct herb brews for mental vigor and to strengthen passion. Inscribe talismans and amulets to gain wealth, eternal youth, or relief from pain. Practice spells to drive away evil, procure your heart's desire, warm the affections of another, or break a troublesome habit. Conduct twelve symbolic rites to honor the ceremonies of the year.

In a world where nature is so often slighted or ignored, this book serves to heighten your awareness of the magic lying beneath the surface, and the powerful ties that exist between mind and matter, even in modern times.

978-1-56718-811-0, 192 pp., 5³⁄₁₆ x 8   **$11.95**

To order, call 1-877-NEW-WRLD
Prices subject to change without notice
Order at Llewellyn.com 24 hours a day, 7 days a week!

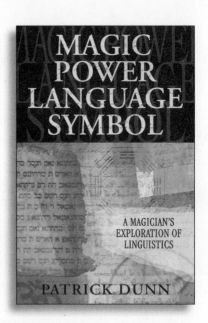

MAGIC
POWER
LANGUAGE
SYMBOL

A MAGICIAN'S
EXPLORATION OF
LINGUISTICS

PATRICK DUNN

Magic, Power, Language, Symbol

A Magician's Exploration of Linguistics

PATRICK DUNN

All forms of magic are linked to language. As a magic practitioner and a linguist, Patrick Dunn illuminates this fascinating relationship and offers breakthrough theories on how and why magic works.

Drawing on linguistics and semiotics (the study of symbols), Dunn illuminates the magical use of language, both theoretically and practically. He poses new theories on the mechanics of magic by analyzing the structure of ritual, written signs and sigils, primal language, incantations across cultures, Qabalah and gematria (Hebrew numerology), and the Enochian vocabulary. This revolutionary paradigm can help magicians understand how sigils and talismans work, compose Enochian spells, speak in tongues for magic, create mantras, work with gematria, use postmodern defixios, and refine their practice in countless other ways.

978-0-7387-1360-1, 288 pp., 6 x 9 **$17.95**

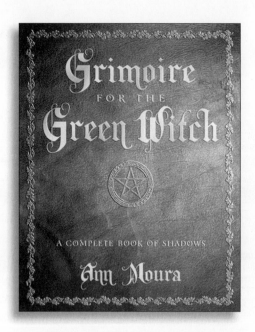

Grimoire
FOR THE
Green Witch

A COMPLETE BOOK OF SHADOWS

Ann Moura

Grimoire for the Green Witch

ANN MOURA

The author of the popular Green Witchcraft series presents her personal book of shadows, designed for you to use just as she uses it—as a working guide to ritual, spells, and divination. It is a book to set on the altar and pass along to the next generation with new notations and entries.

Use *Grimoire for the Green Witch* much like a cookbook. Flip through and select what you need at any given time. It is a reference of circle-casting techniques, traditional rituals for the Esbats and Sabbats, easy-to-make crafts, and a staggering array of correspondences used in creating spells. It is a distillation of Green practice, with room for growth and new inspiration.

978-0-7387-0287-2, 360 pp., 8 x 10   **$19.95**